PAUL
for
EVERYONE

ROMANS

PART 2

CHAPTERS 9-16

ENLARGED PRINT EDITION

NEW TESTAMENT FOR EVERYONE
N. T. Wright

PAUL
for
EVERYONE

ROMANS
PART 2
CHAPTERS 9–16

ENLARGED PRINT EDITION

N. T.
WRIGHT

WJK WESTMINSTER
JOHN KNOX PRESS
LOUISVILLE · KENTUCKY

© 2004 Nicholas Thomas Wright

2015 enlarged print edition
Westminster John Knox Press
Louisville, KY

First published in 2004 in Great Britain by the
Society for Promoting Christian Knowledge
36 Causton Street
London SW1P 4ST
www.spckpublishing.co.uk

and in the United States of America by
Westminster John Knox Press
100 Witherspoon Street
Louisville, KY 40202

15 16 17 18 19 20 21 22 23 24—10 9 8 7 6 5 4 3 2 1

Typeset by Pioneer Associates, Perthshire
Cover design by Lisa Buckley
Cover art: © istockphoto.com

United States Library of Congress Cataloging-in-Publication Data
is on file at the Library of Congress, Washington, D.C.

ISBN: 978-0-664-22912-2 (U.S. edition)
ISBN: 978-0-664-26083-5 (U.S. enlarged print edition)

♾ The paper used in this publication meets the minimum requirements of the American National Standard for Information Sciences—Permanence of Paper for Printed Library Materials, ANSI Z39.48-1992.

Most Westminster John Knox Press books are available at special quantity discounts when purchased in bulk by corporations, organizations, and special-interest groups. For more information, please e-mail SpecialSales@wjkbooks.com.

CONTENTS

CONTENTS

For
Hattie

'In all these things we are completely victorious
through the one who loved us'
Romans 8.37

INTRODUCTION

On the very first occasion when someone stood up in public to tell people about Jesus, he made it very clear: this message is for *everyone*.

It was a great day – sometimes called the birthday of the church. The great wind of God's spirit had swept through Jesus' followers and filled them with a new joy and a sense of God's presence and power. Their leader, Peter, who only a few weeks before had been crying like a baby because he'd lied and cursed and denied even knowing Jesus, found himself on his feet explaining to a huge crowd that something had happened which had changed the world for ever. What God had done for him, Peter, he was beginning to do for the whole world: new life, forgiveness, new hope and power were opening up like spring flowers after a long winter. A new age had begun in which the living God was going to do new things in the world – beginning then and there with the individuals who were listening to him. 'This promise is for *you*,' he said, 'and for your children, and for everyone who is far away' (Acts 2.39). It wasn't just for the person standing next to you. It was for everyone.

Within a remarkably short time this came true to such an extent that the young movement spread throughout much of the known world. And one way in which the *everyone* promise worked out was through the writings of the early Christian leaders. These short works – mostly letters and stories about Jesus – were widely circulated and eagerly read. They were never intended for either a religious or intellectual elite. From the very beginning they were meant for everyone.

That is as true today as it was then. Of course, it matters that some people give time and care to the historical evidence, the meaning of the original words (the early Christians wrote in Greek), and the exact and particular force of what different writers were saying about God, Jesus, the world and themselves. This series is based quite closely on that sort of work. But the point of it all is that the message can get out to everyone, especially to people who wouldn't normally read a book with footnotes and Greek words in it. That's the sort of person for whom these books are written. And that's why there's a glossary, in the back, of the key words that you can't really get along without, with a simple description of what they mean. Whenever you see a word in **bold type** in the text, you can go to the back and remind yourself what's going on.

There are of course many translations of the New Testament available today. The one I offer here is designed for the same kind of reader: one who mightn't necessarily understand the more formal, sometimes even ponderous, tones of some of the standard ones. I have tried, naturally, to keep as close to the original as I can. But my main aim has been to be sure that the words can speak not just to some people, but to everyone.

Paul's letter to the Christians in Rome is his masterpiece. It covers many different topics from many different angles, bringing them all together into a fast-moving and compelling line of thought. Reading it sometimes feels like being swept along in a small boat on a swirling, bubbling river. We need to hold on tight if we're going to stay on board. But if we do, the energy and excitement of it all is unbeatable. The reason is obvious: because Romans is all about the God who, as Paul says, unveils his power and grace through the good news about Jesus. And, as Paul insists again and again, this power and grace is available for everyone who believes. So here it is: Romans for everyone!

Tom Wright

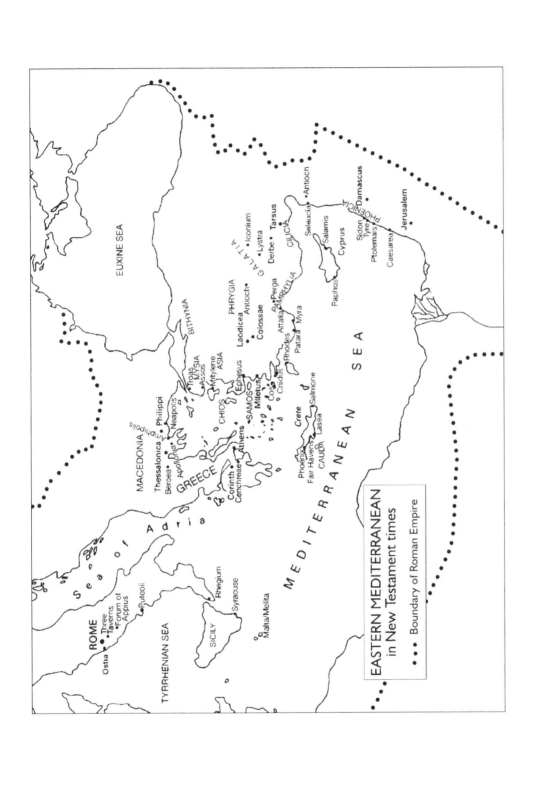

EASTERN MEDITERRANEAN
in New Testament times

••••• Boundary of Roman Empire

ROMANS 9.1–5

The Privileges and Tragedy of Israel

[1]I'm speaking the truth in the Messiah, I'm not lying. I call my conscience as witness, in the Holy Spirit, [2]that I have great sorrow and endless pain in my heart. [3]Left to my own self, I am half inclined to pray that I would be accursed, cut off from the Messiah, on behalf of my own family, my own flesh-and-blood relatives. [4]They are Israelites; the sonship, the glory, the covenants, the giving of the law, the worship and the promises all belong to them. [5]The patriarchs are their ancestors; and it is from them, according to the flesh, that the Messiah has come – who is God over all, blessed for ever, Amen!

This morning's newspaper carries a whole page of correspondence about an ugly fact of modern life: anti-Semitism is on the rise again. Jews have been attacked and threatened, vilified and abused in many cities in our supposedly civilized world. Old lies about the Jews, long since disproved and discredited, have been revived, published and widely circulated. And the letter-writers are asking: could this be because of people's antipathy, not to Jews as such or their Semitic origins and identity, but to the policies of the present Israeli government? This in turn generates a second level of debate, often as bitter as the first: does opposing the policy of a government mean that you are prejudiced against the nation in question? Are you prejudiced because you criticize, or do you criticize because you are prejudiced? It doesn't take much of an argument like that to make most of us throw up our hands in frustration and change the subject. Meanwhile, hatred and violence continue unchecked on their vicious spiral.

This is where we have to begin if we are going to read the next three chapters with any kind of integrity today. Please note, I do not say that we must let our present debates determine what we are prepared to let Paul say. We are here to listen to him, and ponder the meaning of what he says, not to project on to him either the views we want to hear (so that we can enjoy the echo of our own voices) or the views we don't want to hear (so that we can enjoy telling him off for his wrong-headedness). But no Christian today can ignore the fact that for many centuries anti-Semitism flourished across large areas of Christendom, and the church not only did nothing to prevent it but added fuel to the fire by declaring (for instance) that the Jews killed Jesus, despite the insistence of all four **gospels** that it was the Romans. Faced with the present passage, which speaks in every line of God's purposes for Israel, and which proposes a Christian understanding of that difficult and dangerous subject, we must pause and reflect, in sorrow and humility, on how our own **faith** and scriptures have been abused in support of dangerous prejudices. And we must pray for wisdom to do better.

This does not mean – and we would be bound to misunderstand Romans if we thought it did mean – that Paul would support the kind of idea which has been fashionable of late, that everyone must follow their own idea of God, must find their own type of faith, and must be left to their own devices in doing so, since all faiths are of equal value. I think people are gradually coming to realize that not all beliefs are healthy and life-giving, and that not all lifestyles are equally honouring to ourselves as human beings, let alone to the God in whose image we are made. But what Paul is doing in this passage goes beyond that debate. He

2

wants to do two things which people still have a hard time putting together. He wants to affirm, passionately, that God really did choose the Jews and equip them to be his people for the world. And he wants to affirm, equally passionately, that Jesus of Nazareth really was and is Israel's **Messiah**. Indeed, the second depends on the first: unless you believe in God's unique call to Israel, you miss the point of believing in a Messiah altogether. The Messiah comes – as Paul hints by putting him at the climax of the list of Israel's privileges in verses 4 and 5 – as the culmination of God's work, in line with all the privileges and promises of old.

That, of course, is the problem, for Paul and for us. For Paul it meant the constant mental and emotional turmoil of believing that Jesus was the promised Messiah and knowing that most of his fellow Jews rejected this belief. He was like someone driving in convoy who takes a particular turn in the road and then watches in horror as most of the other cars take the other fork. They think he's wrong; he thinks they're wrong. What is worse, he really does believe that the road he has taken is the only road to the fulfilment of God's great promises. What will happen to them? Why did they go that way, ignoring the signs that made him take the other fork? Unless we recognize that Paul thought like that, we won't understand why he is so sad or why he thinks of praying the desperate prayer he mentions in verse 3.

Sadness, indeed, is what we find here. Paul's description of his state of heart in verses 1, 2 and 3 reminds me of the sort of thing people say when they are in the depths of grief, or suffering from severe depression. When you're in that state, everything that happens, every word you hear, every sight you see, is coloured by the fact that something has gone desperately wrong. You can't forget it for a moment. Paul was a master of writing and speaking, and he knows exactly the effect this sudden outburst will produce. The end of Romans 8 was and is glorious, meant to lead us to one of the highest points of Christian celebration and reflection. But in the present life such moments are always balanced by the sorrowful realization of the dark shadow which the bright light now casts. And that realization is meant to lead us, too, into prayer, humility, reflection and wisdom.

That reflection must begin by noticing that all the privileges Paul mentions in verses 4 and 5 are things he has already mentioned in the first eight chapters of the letter, not least in the majestic chapter that has just closed. He has declared that all who belong to the Messiah are God's adopted children. They rejoice in the hope of God's glory. The **covenant** promises have been fulfilled in the Messiah, and are now theirs by right. What the **law** could not do, God has done, and those in the Messiah now benefit from it. They are the ones who are learning the true worship, of loving God and obeying him in faith (1.5; 8.28). They inherit the promises made to the patriarchs. And they are, of course, defined as the people of the Messiah, despite the fact that most of them are not ethnically Jewish.

We have met this theme as well, of course, over and over again in the earlier chapters of Romans. People have often imagined that chapters 9—11 are a kind of bracket, an appendix, tackling a different subject from the rest of the letter. But that only shows how badly Romans as a whole has been misread. The whole letter is about the way God is fulfilling his ancient promises in and through Jesus, and what this will mean in practice. This inevitably raises the question of a proper Christian attitude towards those Jews who do not accept Jesus as Messiah. Now we begin to find – well, not an easy answer, and some would say not an 'answer' in the satisfying sense at all; rather, a way of thinking, which is rooted in a way of praying, which is rooted in love and grief. Perhaps, at the start of the twenty-first century, we can hope that Christian people will ponder these things more deeply and learn fresh wisdom.

As we do, we may just note that Paul has set a pattern, at the end of verse 5, for what is to come. The Messiah is from the Jewish people 'according to the flesh', in his flesh-and-blood identity. But he is also the Lord of all: the incarnate God who claims the allegiance of people of every race and nation. That is the point of tension, the fault line which Paul's argument will now straddle. The Jews really are the people of the Messiah, but they are that 'according to the flesh'. The Messiah really does belong to them, but only in the 'fleshly' sense; and he also belongs to the whole world as its rightful Lord. We are reminded of what Paul said at the beginning of the whole letter, in 1.3–4, and of the way that statement worked out in the following chapters. Something similar is going to happen this time as well. To ponder all this in prayer, and to refrain from rash or prejudiced judgments as we do so, is the only possible way forward for mature Christian reflection.

ROMANS 9.6–13

Abraham's Two Families

⁶But it can't be the case that God's word has failed! Not all who are from Israel, you see, are in fact Israel. ⁷Nor is it the

case that all the children count as 'seed of Abraham'. No: 'in Isaac shall your seed be named'. [8]That means that it isn't the flesh-and-blood children who are God's children; rather, it is the children of the promise who will be calculated as 'seed'. [9]This was what the promise said, you see: 'Around this time I shall return, and Sarah shall have a son.'

[10]And that's not all. The same thing happened when Rebekah conceived children by one man, our ancestor Isaac. [11]When they had not yet been born, and had done nothing either good or bad – so that what God had in mind in making his choice might come to pass, [12]not because of works but because of the one who calls – it was said to her, 'the elder shall serve the younger'. [13]As the Bible says, 'I loved Jacob, but I hated Esau.'

When you walk or drive through unfamiliar territory, you have to rely on the map. It is the bottom line. If you find yourself somewhere you didn't expect, you scratch your head, get out the map again, and figure out where you went wrong. You mistook *that* turning for *this* one . . . so you took the road that went over *there* instead of over *here* . . . so no wonder you've landed up on the wrong side of the river. You'll have to go back and start again from the place where you made the mistake. It is of course possible in theory that the map might be wrong. Map-makers are fallible human beings like the rest of us. But if that's so, then you really are lost. There's nothing you can trust.

What we see in this passage and the next ones, right through to verse 29, is Paul going back to the beginning of the map and starting again. Jewish thinkers in his day often retold the story of Israel, beginning with Abraham or even with Adam, in order to explain the whole sequence of God's actions in their history up to the present day and even beyond. Paul is doing something similar. Here he tells, from one surprising angle, the story of Abraham, Isaac and Jacob – and of Ishmael and Esau as well – in order to explain what the map (God's word of promise) had in mind all along. He had misread it, he now believes, and is eager to help others who had misread it in the same way.

As far as Paul is concerned, the map, the scriptures which he believed to be God's **word**, could not be wrong. You can hold in your mind the theoretical possibility that they may have got it wrong – that God might have made a blunder, or changed his mind, or simply been unable to carry out what he had intended. But if that is so, you really are lost. There's nothing and nobody you can trust. Everything Paul has said so far in the letter, based as it is on God's promises, would then be worthless.

Many people today, of course, would cheerfully say that if there is a God, he (or she, or it) seems to have made all kinds of blunders. The world is indeed chaotic, they say. There's no sense to it except the law of the jungle. Lots of people live on that basis. That is one reason why the world is in a mess; the theory becomes a self-fulfilling prophecy. But Paul is committed, and Christianity like Judaism is committed, to a different belief: that it is we who have made the blunders, and that to accuse God of them is sheer projection, like a drunkard stumbling into a ditch and accusing the road-makers of tripping him up. Or like someone holding the map upside down and then, upon arriving at a dead end, accusing the map-makers of incompetence. The question of the faithfulness and justice of the one true God – the question all thinking humans must come to sooner or later – is on the table at this point, and though we may not like what we hear there is no turning back.

What did Paul discover when he went back to the map, to the ancient stories of the patriarchs, and the promises God made to them? Just this: that from the very beginning God seems to have decided to work his strange purposes by means not only of choosing one family from of the whole human race, but *by continuing that practice within the chosen family itself*. This, in fact, would have been uncontroversial among Jewish thinkers of his day, as far as the first three generations were concerned; everyone knew that God had chosen Isaac rather than Ishmael, and Jacob rather than Esau. (Paul assumes his readers know the story of the book of Genesis, in which Abraham had two sons, Isaac by his wife Sarah and Ishmael by Sarah's maid Hagar, and Isaac had twin sons, Esau and Jacob, by his wife Rebekah.) What Paul is going to suggest, though, is that the principle on which God was operating goes deeper and further than his contemporaries, and he himself, had realized.

The first point is that the practice of selection, of God working his purposes through some and not others, was intended to continue past Jacob and on into the subsequent history of Israel. It had continued, in fact, right down to the point where the **Messiah** had carried Israel's destiny all by himself. When Paul arrives at last at 10.4, the central point of the argument of these chapters, we realize that this was where the whole story had been heading. God's purpose was to act *within history* to deal with the problem of evil, but this could only be done by employing a people who were themselves part of the problem, until the time was ripe for God's own son to emerge from their midst and, all alone, to take their destiny upon himself.

8

The second point is that this principle of selection, of God choosing to carry forward his plan by some rather than others, was done without regard for the moral character of the people involved. Paul perhaps has in mind at this point the regular Jewish proposal that God chose Abraham because he was a man of outstanding moral and spiritual ability, with the implication that the status of Israel as God's chosen people was similarly dependent on their being morally and spiritually superior to the rest of the human race. Paul spent quite a bit of time earlier in the letter disproving that suggestion (without suggesting for a moment that Israel's special status didn't matter). Now he returns to the point in order to tell the long, winding story of God's dealings with Israel from Abraham to his own day.

The main thing he wants to say at this stage, from the start, is that the promises God made to Abraham and Sarah, and then to Isaac and Rebekah, always envisaged this process of selection. God's promise would be carried forward by the 'seed of Abraham'. But when you examine the promises closely (Paul is quoting here from Genesis 21.12; 18.10, 14 and 25.23, throwing in Malachi 1.2–3 for good measure), it turns out that 'the seed of Abraham' was never intended to include every single physical child descended from the first patriarch. Sarah's children, not Hagar's, would count; the promise would relate to Isaac, not Ishmael.

On reading verses 6, 7 and 8, you can imagine someone saying, 'Well, that's fine; it's obviously because Sarah was Abraham's wife, whereas Hagar, Ishmael's mother, was simply a servant-girl.' But Paul won't allow that. The next generation proves the point: Esau and Jacob were twins, sharing not only the same mother, but the same single moment of conception. And yet God's purpose, announced before they were born, was that the line of promise should run through Jacob rather than Esau – a word reaffirmed roughly a thousand years later, as the prophet Malachi reflected on what had happened to the descendants of the two brothers in the subsequent centuries.

Many people feel uneasy reading these verses, and that uneasiness comes to boiling point at verse 13. Hasn't Paul managed to rescue God from the charge of incompetence, of failing to do what he promised, only to land him instead into a much worse one, of flagrant favouritism and injustice? Paul is as well aware of this question as we are, as the very next verse will show. But we should reflect, as well, on what Malachi himself meant when he said that God loved Jacob but hated Esau. There was no question that God had done remarkable things for Israel, Jacob's family, while Edom, the family of Esau, had collapsed into insignificance. But the point the prophet was making was that this now increased the responsibility, and culpability, of Israel. The thrust was not, You are special so you can sit back and take it easy. It was always, You are special, so why are you taking God for granted, failing to honour him, and ignoring your call to carry forward his purposes? God's choice never results in easy, arrogant, automatic superiority. Much is expected of those to whom much is given.

ROMANS 9.14–24

God's Purpose and Justice

[14]So what are we going to say? Is God unjust? Certainly not! [15]He says to Moses, you see, 'I will have mercy on those

on whom I will have mercy, and I will pity those I will pity.' ¹⁶So, then, it doesn't depend on human willing, or on human effort; it depends on God who shows mercy. ¹⁷For the Bible says to Pharaoh: 'This is why I have raised you up, to show my power in you, and so that my name may be proclaimed in all the earth.' ¹⁸So, then, he has mercy on the one he wants, and he hardens the one he wants.

¹⁹You will say to me, then, 'So why does he still blame people? Who can stand against his purpose?' ²⁰Are you, a mere human being, going to answer God back? 'Surely the clay won't say to the potter, "Why did you make me like this?"' ²¹Doesn't the potter have authority over the clay, so that he can make from the same lump one vessel for honour, and another for dishonour? ²²Supposing God wanted to demonstrate his anger and make known his power, and for that reason put up very patiently with the vessels of anger created for destruction, ²³in order at the same time to make known the riches of his glory on the vessels of mercy, the ones he prepared in advance for glory – ²⁴including us, whom he called not only from among the Jews but also from among the Gentiles?

I was never much good at pottery at school. I enjoyed the feel of the clay, but it never quite did what I wanted it to. I did succeed in making one or two small dishes, including an ashtray (that dates it, because the only person I would have made that for was my father, and he gave up smoking in, I think, 1963). But I never managed the much higher art of real pottery, making mugs, jugs or vases with a potter's wheel. I remain envious of people who can do that kind of thing.

What I do remember, though, is the sign that hung on the wall of the large room at school where we did pottery and various other crafts. 'If thou hast a piece of earthenware,' it said, 'consider that it is a piece of earthenware, and as such very likely to be broken. Be not thou therefore grieved if this should come to pass.' In other words, if your best friend drops your new pot and breaks it, don't punch him on the nose.

But there are two quite different stages in pottery. The second stage, once the pot is shaped, is firing and glazing. That finishes the job, and from then on you have either a whole pot or (if somebody smashes it) a broken one. The earlier stage, though, is quite different. The potter shapes the clay on the wheel. I've watched it done many times since those early days, and it remains one of the lovely human creative arts, with potter and clay responding to one another. Woe betide the potter who simply tries to force the clay to do things it won't do (imagine someone trying to make a square jug on a potter's wheel, for instance). But woe betide . . . well, the other half of the statement brings us back to Paul.

And to one of his most controversial statements. How can he imply that human beings are just like clay, waiting for God to mould them this way or that? Many people have become angry at this point with what they see, not as a broken pot, but a broken argument. Has Paul perhaps (to change the metaphor) painted himself into a corner?

No, he hasn't. What we often miss when we read a passage like this is the underlying story he is telling, the story that emerges when we notice the quotations in the passage and see where they are coming from. The passage about the potter and the clay is taken from Isaiah 29.16 and 45.9, with echoes of 64.8 and also of Jeremiah 18.1–6. All of these are worth looking up and reflecting on. They tell of a stage in Israel's history when God was struggling with rebellious Israel, like a potter working with clay that simply wouldn't go into the right shape. The image of potter and clay was not designed to speak in general terms about human beings as lifeless lumps of clay, over against God as the only living, thinking being; it was designed to speak very specifically about God's purpose in choosing and calling Israel, and about what would happen if Israel, like a lump of clay, failed to respond to the gentle moulding of his hands.

At that point God's purpose must go forward, whether or not Israel is obedient to its vocation. We are back once more with what Paul was talking about at the beginning of chapter 3. Indeed, the sequence of questions in our present chapter (in verses 6, 14 and 19) reflects quite closely the similar sequence in 3.1–9. We cannot simply reject this passage as though Paul is talking about God and humanity in the abstract. He is talking about God's purposes not only *with* Israel but, much more importantly, *through* Israel.

What were the purposes which God wanted to put into effect through Israel? As we have seen, the answer is that Israel was called to be the light of the world, the people through whom God would speak his **word** of promise and new creation to all the nations. But the prophets themselves saw that Israel as it stood was rebelling, like a lump of clay challenging the potter and demanding to be made into a different shape.

The point Paul is making here, indeed throughout Romans 9—11, is that this is happening at the first stage of the pottery procedure. God has not yet arrived at the moment when the clay goes in the oven and comes out solid, so that from then on the only options are either to stay the way it is or to be smashed to pieces. Fortunately for

Israel and the world, when Israel rebelled the process was still at the moulding stage. And if the pot is spoiled at that stage, of course the potter has the right (indeed, if God is the potter, he has the obligation) to rework and remould it into a new shape. What would we prefer? That he would throw the clay out and start again with entirely new clay? That question lies at the heart of the puzzle of God, the world, Israel, Jesus and the church.

The present passage, reaching its climax in this image of potter and clay, is in fact a continuation of the story which Paul started in verse 6 – the story, that is, of Israel in the Old Testament. We move from Abraham, Isaac and Jacob to the time of the **Exodus** from Egypt, with Moses leading the people out despite the opposition of Pharaoh. From there we come forwards into the period of the prophets, warning Israel that it was going off course from God's purpose and that, if this persisted, God would have to remould and remake Israel in a new way, not because God was forgetting his promises but precisely because he was being faithful to them.

It is this ongoing purpose, despite the fact of Israel's rebellion, that causes God to declare to Moses that he will proceed with his plan for the Exodus even though the people have made the golden calf, amounting to a declaration of independence from the true God. That is the setting for the passage in Exodus 33 which Paul quotes in verse 15. It then appears (verse 17) that God is doing with Israel itself what he did with Pharaoh, the king of Egypt who withstood God's purposes to bring Israel out of slavery. God works even within that human rebellion and arrogance to bring about an even more glorious work of rescue, revealing his power, and gaining a worldwide reputation for performing

14

extraordinary acts of judgment and mercy. But the angle of vision is always forwards. You only understand this or that particular incident in the light of what God intends to do through it, the ultimate purposes for which God called Israel in the first place.

Where does this leave the story of Israel on the one hand, and Paul's developing argument on the other?

It brings the story of Israel up to the point where, in the historical and prophetic writings of the Old Testament, Israel goes into **exile** in order to be reshaped by God; where, in other words, the potter remoulds the clay. The Jewish scriptures themselves (this is Paul's underlying point) speak of God rightly and properly acting to take forward his eventual plan, even though this will mean reshaping Israel quite drastically. The alternative, after all, would seem to be that God would simply ignore Israel's rebellion and proceed with an automatic 'favoured-nation clause' which Paul has already firmly ruled out in chapter 2 – or that God would scrap the plan and the promises altogether, which again is ruled out by God's own character. God will be faithful to his purpose and promise, even if all humans prove false.

Paul's developing argument has got to the point where he has established that God has the right to remould his people. He now begins to suggest that he has done so in fact, not least by calling **Gentiles** to share as full and equal members. This is a drastic and unprecedented new point within the story of Israel as normally told in Paul's world. Somehow, he now sees the torch being passed from a group consisting only of Jews (a selection from within Abraham's physical family) to a group consisting of Jews and Gentiles together. Within the argument of Romans, of course, we

15

are used to this point. Paul has emphasized it over and over in chapters 2, 3 and 4. But within the present line of thought verse 24 is startling indeed.

Paul will develop the point in the following passages. For the moment we should simply note that the idea of a 'vessel of mercy' doesn't mean so much a vessel which receives mercy, but a vessel through which God brings mercy to others.

ROMANS 9.25–29

God Calls a Remnant

[25]This is what he says in Hosea,

I will call 'not my people' 'my people';
and 'not beloved' I will call 'beloved'.
[26]And in the place where it was said to them,
'You are not my people',
there they will be called 'sons of the living God'.

[27]Isaiah cries out, concerning Israel,

Even if the number of Israel's sons are like the sand by
the sea,
only a remnant shall be saved;
[28]for the Lord will bring judgment on the earth,
complete and decisive.

[29]As Isaiah said in an earlier passage,

If the Lord of Hosts had not left us seed,
we would have become like Sodom, and been made
like Gomorrah.

The Beatles once recorded a song called 'Nowhere Man'. It grew out of a casual, dismissive remark one of them had made about somebody they'd just met: 'He's a real "nowhere man".' It was meant as a scornful put-down, and if the person they were referring to had ever heard it, it would have hurt. Imagine calling someone 'Mr Nobody', or 'Little Miss Nobody-Loves-Me'. It's the sort of thing children might say to each other in a malicious mood. Give someone a label which writes them off, and watch them squirm.

The prophets knew all about giving people names – and particularly about giving Israel names, names which reflected what God was thinking about them. These were not cheap put-down remarks, though; they were serious words designed to make Israel stop in its tracks and think again about what they were doing. The first two chapters of the prophet Hosea are full of this kind of thing, and Paul draws on two key promises from that passage. He quotes them in reverse order, beginning with Hosea 2.23, where the prophet declares to the Israelites that God will receive them back again after rejecting them. They were called 'not my people', but now they are to be called 'my people'. They were called 'not beloved', but now God will call them 'beloved'. Then he quotes the earlier passage, Hosea 1.10: in the place where you were called 'not my people', you will be called 'sons of the living God'.

What is Paul saying with these (to us) somewhat obscure, though clearly dramatic, quotations? He is continuing to tell the story of Israel, the story which began with Abraham and the other patriarchs, which continued through the **Exodus**, and which now reaches the period of the prophets. Paul's point, made here in poetic fashion, is in essence quite simple: the prophets themselves promised that God would make Israel pass through a period of judgment in order then to come out into salvation. First Israel had to hear, and bear, the name 'not my people', before they could again be called 'my people'.

Paul's point, yet once more, is that God has indeed been faithful to his promises. He has not gone back on his **word**. He said he would have to whittle Israel down to a remnant, and that's what he has now done. To imagine that Israel could be vindicated as it stood – that all Jews would automatically be classified as true 'children of Abraham' – would be to ignore what Israel's own scriptures had been saying all along. The problem of Jewish unbelief is not, then, the problem of God failing to keep his word, but the problem of Israel not hearing what that word had been saying.

The idea of a 'remnant', which I just mentioned, comes in the passage Paul quotes next, this time from Isaiah. To get the full flavour of this, remember that Paul is rounding off here the train of thought he began at 9.6, where he was talking about Abraham and his family, his 'seed', those who are 'children of God' (9.8) and not merely 'children according to the flesh'. The quotation from Hosea looks back to the 'children of God' passage. Now the quotation from Isaiah 10.22 picks up on one of the best-known promises to Abraham (Genesis 22.17), that his seed would be like the sand on the seashore. Well, says Isaiah, that may indeed come to pass; the number of Israel's sons according to the flesh may well grow to that size; but even if they do, only a remnant will be saved. Only some of them will find their way into God's new age, the time when mercy returns after cataclysmic judgment. Paul adds to his quotation from Isaiah 10 another one, this time from Isaiah 28.22, which insists that the YHWH, the Lord of hosts, will make a complete and decisive judgment on the earth. God must put the world to rights, and when he does so Israel can look for no special favours. What God will do, however, is ensure that a 'remnant' is rescued.

What is this 'remnant'? Paul is going to come back to the idea in chapter 11, but from the way it appears in other Jewish writings around this time we can say at least this. Many Jewish groups in Paul's day took it for granted that, when God finally acted to judge and save, by no means all ethnic Jews would be among those rescued. Many had rebelled against God and his word, and had appeared to want no part in his salvation. Devout Jews, observing this, picked up on these promises and declared that God was cutting Israel down to size, pruning his people quite drastically. Sometimes (as in the **Dead Sea Scrolls**) people thought of this in terms of a small minority who were somehow spared the judgment. Paul sees it, rather, as those who are brought through the judgment and out the other side. That will be the foundation of the fresh story he will tell in chapter 11, of how the present 'remnant' of believing Jews can be increased.

The final quotation from Isaiah (1.9) points in the same direction, and once more ties in to the Abraham story. Sodom and Gomorrah were the cities of the plain, now buried beneath the Dead Sea. They were destroyed in a great act of judgment, while Abraham, whose nephew Lot had gone to live in Sodom, looked on from a distance (Genesis 19.27–28). Isaiah looks back to this story and declares that if God hadn't left them a remnant, Israel as a whole, Abraham's own family, would have gone the same way. Paul actually changes the word 'remnant', used by

Isaiah here, to 'seed', in order to tie it in to the discussion of 9.7–8.

The passage is thus complex and dense, but its general drift is clear. Paul is rounding off what we might call 'Israel's story so far' by quoting Old Testament prophets to show that what has now happened, with most Jews remaining outside God's renewed people and only a remnant inside it, is exactly what God had said would happen. He has made his main point: God's word has not failed. On the contrary, it has come all too uncomfortably true. And the second question he has to deal with, whether God is just or unjust, has been addressed in the process: God has had to deal with Israel, not as a blank slate, but as a rebellious people deserving of judgment. When that judgment falls, Israel has no reason to complain. In fact, God has been merciful in rescuing a remnant, despite universal sinfulness.

In the course of this long argument (9.6–29), Paul has said a great many things which we need to ponder carefully. In particular, we must remember that he is discussing ethnic Israel as the people of the **Messiah**, albeit 'according to the flesh'. What he says in this passage belongs closely with several earlier parts of the letter, two in particular.

First, in chapter 3 he explains how God must go ahead with his promised plan even if Israel proves unfaithful. The way God will do this is by sending Jesus as the faithful Israelite, the Messiah through whose death and **resurrection** God will fulfil his saving purpose. Second, in chapter 7 he describes how, through the **law**, sin gathered itself to its full height within Israel, in order that, through the death of the Messiah, sin could finally be condemned as it deserved.

These two passages, taken together, point in the direction of chapter 9. Here, Israel finds itself called to a particular, and very strange, role in God's purposes – that of being apparently cast away in order that God's powerful plan of salvation can go forwards. Paul never spells this theme out more fully. But it seems as though he is looking at his fellow Jews – at himself, indeed – as people called, whether or not they understand or co-operate, to be part of the saving plan which reaches its climax in the 'casting away' of the Messiah himself on the cross. His apparently harsh words are to be understood in the light of the even harsher reality of what happened to Jesus. This will enable him, in what now follows, to explain his continuing desire that more Jews should in fact find God's way of salvation.

ROMANS 9.30—10.4

Israel, the Nations and the Messiah

[30]What then shall we say? That the nations, who were not aspiring towards covenant membership, have obtained covenant membership, but it is a covenant membership based on faith. [31]Israel meanwhile, though eager for the law which defined the covenant, did not attain to the law. [32]Why not? Because they did not pursue it on the basis of faith, but as though it was on the basis of works. They have stumbled over the stumbling stone, [33]as the Bible says,

Look: I am placing in Sion
a stone that will make people stumble,
a rock that will trip people up;
and the one who believes in him
will never be put to shame.

21

10.1My dear family, the longing of my heart, and my prayer to God on their behalf, is for their salvation. 2I can testify on their behalf that they have a zeal for God; but it is not based on knowledge. 3They were ignorant, you see, of God's covenant faithfulness, and they were trying to establish a covenant status of their own; so they didn't submit to God's faithfulness. 4The Messiah, you see, is the goal of the law, so that covenant membership may be available for all who believe.

One of the things I have to do in my job is to encourage people who are building new churches or other premises for worship, outreach, child care and so on. Often this involves being there when the first bit of the building is done, to pray over the foundation stone and ask God to bless both the building itself and all the work that will go on within it.

Usually what's called the 'foundation stone' isn't actually part of the foundation itself. If it was, nobody would be able to see it, because it would be some way underground. So another stone, a little way above ground, is designated as the 'foundation stone', often with an inscription to say that the building was dedicated on such-and-such a date, and so on.

But supposing the foundation stone was placed right at ground level, so that it was literally the visible base of the coming building. And supposing that it was standing there, after the ceremony but before any more of the building had gone up. And supposing someone walking past at the dead of night didn't notice it was there. The stone that had been intended as the foundation of a building would trip them up.

It's an odd picture, but it's more or less exactly what Paul has in mind in 9.33. He is bringing together two passages in Isaiah, both about a 'stone' which God will place on the ground.

In Isaiah 28.16 the stone is the foundation of the new **Temple** that's yet to be built. It looks, in the passage, as though what the prophet has in mind is actually the coming King who will be the human foundation for the great community focused on the Temple. In Isaiah 8.14, however, the prophet declares to God's rebellious people that God will place in front of them a stone that people will stumble over or trip up on. This is part of the judgment that will fall. Even when God does something good, even when he provides for his people, those who are bent on rebellion will find it a trap.

But in Isaiah 28, the prophet ends with a promise which Paul applies to both ideas together: anyone who believes in him will not be put to shame. The words Paul uses could mean 'in it' rather than, or perhaps as well as, 'in him', but it comes to the same thing. The 'stone' in both passages seems to refer to the coming King, and certainly that is how Paul wants us to read it.

By bringing these two passages together, Paul has cleverly used a combined biblical text to say that now, once more in fulfilment of scripture rather than as a change of plan on God's part, the foundation of God's new 'building' has been laid – but that those who don't believe in him, in the **Messiah** who is the foundation, will trip over this 'stone' and fall flat on their faces. He is still explaining how it is that Israel's substantial failure to believe in Jesus as Messiah, either during Jesus' public career or during the present time of missionary work, does not represent a thwarting of God's plan or a change of God's mind, but rather an unexpected fulfilment, albeit comprehensible only with hindsight, of what God had planned all along.

This double quotation from Isaiah stands at the middle of the present passage, which is itself more or less central to the whole of chapters 9—11. We are here at the heart of Paul's argument: like a guide on a walk, he is explaining where the journey has now got to. Having followed through the story of Abraham and Israel (9.6–29), we have arrived at the point where we can see what's been going on. **Gentiles** have been coming into the **covenant** family God promised to Abraham, while a good many Jews have been going about things the wrong way and so have failed to have the **faith** which alone marks out the members of that true family.

This discussion relates closely to two previous passages in the letter, both of which should be in mind at this point. In 3.21—4.25 Paul spelled out the way in which Abraham's true family consists of all those, Jew and Gentile alike, who believe in the **gospel** of Jesus and so share Abraham's faith, the one and only badge of family membership. This, Paul explained, was the revelation, or the unveiling, of God's own covenant faithfulness, God's justice, the divine plan to put the world to rights. Then, in 7.1—8.11, Paul explains how the **law** actually lured Israel into a deliberate trap, becoming the place where sin increased to its full height, in order that the Messiah, representing Israel, could take the weight of that sin on to himself and, in his death, become the place where it was condemned once and for all.

Paul is now drawing on these previous passages in order to say, within the flow of thought of chapters 9, 10 and 11, that the story of God and Israel has reached its climax with the coming, and the death and **resurrection**, of the Messiah.

This then explains the extraordinary fact that Gentiles, nations which had not been called by the creator God, have been flooding into the covenant family, while Jews, the physical family of Abraham, have in effect turned their backs on it because the means they were using to consolidate their membership were counter-productive.

Here we meet a problem we noted earlier in the letter. One of the key technical terms in this letter is the word I've translated 'covenant membership' in 9.30, 'covenant faithfulness' in its first occurrence in 10.3, 'covenant status' in its second occurrence in that verse, 'faithfulness' on its third occurrence, and then 'covenant membership' again in 10.4. Why on earth would a translator do something like that?

The problem is that the word, often translated 'righteousness', and sometimes 'uprightness' or 'justice', really does mean all of those things and more. Paul is exploiting it, in a way that's very hard to do in English, to get to the heart of what he wants to say, which centres on the following three things.

First, God really has been faithful to the covenant. What has happened – specifically, the coming of the Messiah, and the reaction to him from Jews and Gentiles – is what God had in mind all along, even though Israel hadn't understood this. This misunderstanding was itself, it appears, actually part of the plan.

Second, membership in God's covenant family, that is, membership in the people God promised to Abraham, is marked out by faith alone, not works of the Jewish law. This is why Gentiles who believe the gospel are counted as full members.

Third, Paul's fellow Jews were doing their best (as he himself had done prior to his conversion) to use the law as a badge of covenant membership. They were relying on their performance of its commands to demonstrate that they were the true children of Abraham. But the law was never meant to work that way. That's why they have tripped over the 'stone', the Messiah who is the foundation of the true family. That's why, too, they have remained ignorant of God's covenant purposes, and the fact that he had been faithful to his promises when he sent Jesus as the Messiah (10.3, 4). 'The Messiah is the goal of the Law': this is where God's strange purposes had been heading all along.

This is one of the crucial moments in all of Paul's writing. If we get our heads round it we will understand a good many other things too. But we shouldn't miss, in the middle of Paul's visionary glimpse of how God's purposes had reached their climax, his deeply personal prayer, echoing what he had said at the start of chapter 9. The longing of his heart, and his prayer to God for his fellow Jews, is that they might be saved (10.1). Much of the rest of the section, to the end of chapter 11, is devoted to explaining how that might now come about.

ROMANS 10.5–13

The Fulfilment of the Covenant

[5]Moses writes, you see, about the covenant membership defined by the law, that 'the person who performs the law's commands shall live in them.' [6]But the *faith*-based covenant membership puts it like this: 'Don't say in your heart, Who shall go up to heaven?' (in other words, to bring the Messiah down), [7]or, 'Who shall go down into the depths?' (in other words, to bring the Messiah up from the dead).

⁸But what does it say? 'The word is near you, in your mouth and in your heart' (that is, the word of faith which we proclaim); ⁹because if you profess with your mouth that Jesus is Lord, and believe in your heart that God raised him from the dead, you will be saved. ¹⁰Why? Because the way to covenant membership is by believing with the heart, and the way to salvation is by professing with the mouth. ¹¹The Bible says, you see, 'Everyone who believes in him will not be put to shame.' ¹²For there is no distinction between Jew and Greek, since the same Lord is Lord of all, and is rich towards all who call upon him. ¹³'All who call upon the name of the Lord', you see, 'will be saved.'

Edward Elgar was the greatest English composer of the late nineteenth and early twentieth century. Among his many works, perhaps the best known is the *Enigma Variations*. As the second word of its name implies, it is a set of variations on a theme, and Elgar devised each variation in such a way as to paint a portrait, in the music, of one or other of his many friends. Indeed, he wrote a dedication to the work: 'To my friends, pictured within'.

But the 'Enigma' of the title is itself enigmatic. Elgar hinted that the theme he had chosen could itself be combined with a well-known popular tune. To this day, however, there is no agreement as to what this tune might be.

Clearly, though, part of the enjoyment of listening to a set of variations is discovering, within the original melody, hints of something new, which the variations can then bring out. Many musicians have produced delightful works by this means, and many writers have done the same. This, in fact, is what Paul is doing in the present passage.

Recognizing this, and working out what he's up to, is the only way to unravel what otherwise remains quite a dense and daunting bit of theology.

The main 'tune' he's working with is Deuteronomy 30. It's a spectacular passage full of promise and life. Many Jews of Paul's day had studied it carefully. They were hoping to find out what God was going to do for them after all the years they had suffered at the hands of pagan nations. But why would they study *this* passage to find out *that*?

Deuteronomy 28, 29 and 30 come near the end of Moses' long charge to the Israelites before they enter the promised land. These chapters tell a story of what is going to happen to Israel in the days to come. If Israel keeps God's commandments, God promises blessings; if they don't, he warns of curses to come. What's more, Moses solemnly predicts that Israel will disobey, and so incur the curses. And the worst of the curses is that they will be driven out of the promised land, sent off into **exile**. That's what chapters 28 and 29 are all about.

But then Deuteronomy 30 has a fresh **word**, a further promise to which God commits himself (that's the point of a '**covenant**'). When Israel has gone into exile, they might suppose that everything is finished; but God promises that if they turn back to him even while they are in exile, he will rescue them. More specifically, he promises to transform them, to change their hearts, so that they can at last keep his **law** the way he always intended. It won't be a matter of people needing to climb up to **heaven** to get at the law; they won't have to go across the sea to find it. *It* will come and find *them*! Then exile will be over; the curse will be undone; Israel will be saved.

But what will this look like when it happens? How will Israel, when oppressed and exiled by foreign nations, know what to do, how to come by this new dispensation of the law? This question gnawed away at Jewish thinkers in the centuries before Paul's time, as many of them believed they were still suffering the curses of Deuteronomy 29, with foreigners ruling over them. They longed for this promise of covenant renewal, including the **circumcision** of the heart, to come true, so that Israel could truly love the Lord (30.6) and be saved by him. So this 'tune', this theme of blessings, curses and then the strange transformation and salvation, was the subject of a good many 'variations' as different thinkers struggled to see how their own generation could be the one to inherit the promises.

In particular, we have two other texts, not so well known as the Bible itself, but important because they were written by Jewish thinkers within a century or so of Paul, in which we can see this 'tune' being taken up and played in new ways. In both cases the writers see their own time as the moment when Deuteronomy 30 is about to be fulfilled. The covenant is to be renewed at last, Israel is to be restored to its former glory, and God's people will keep the law from the heart.

One of these texts is in the third chapter of the book called 'Baruch', in the 'Apocrypha' (Jewish books written between the time of the Old and New Testaments). There the writer expounds Deuteronomy 30 in terms of 'wisdom', drawing on other ancient Israelite traditions like those in Proverbs 8. What Deuteronomy was talking about, the writer indicates, was the need for Israel to get the true wisdom which nobody can find by going up into heaven or across the sea. God alone will give it to Israel; when he does, Israel will be restored, saved, rescued from her long exile.

The second of these texts is in one of the **Dead Sea Scrolls**, the one known as 'Some Works of the Law'. This writer, too, believes that his own generation is to be the one for whom Deuteronomy 30 comes true, but he sees the 'law' which God sends to his people, transforming them and rescuing them, not in terms of 'wisdom' but in the form of a collection of special laws which he hopes will be observed in the **Temple** in Jerusalem. These, he says, will be the true marks of God's covenant people, the badge they will wear in the **present age** to show already that they are the people whom God will vindicate at the final day of judgment when it comes.

In both of these texts – strange, no doubt, to us today, but fitting in very well with the way people were reading Deuteronomy in the time of Jesus and Paul – we see the same ideas coming out. First, Israel is indeed still suffering the curses of Deuteronomy 29, separated from God and ruled over by foreign nations. Second, God has now provided the way for Israel to return, to be transformed, to be saved. Third, this way consists of God giving to Israel a fresh gift of grace, which will be like the original law only now in a new way – 'wisdom' in the one case, special regulations for worship in the other. Fourth, those who embrace this new way will be marked out *in the present* as the people whom God will save, vindicate, and declare to be his people *in the future*.

This is exactly what Paul says in this passage, with the remarkable difference that instead of 'wisdom', or new regulations for worship, Paul is of course talking about Jesus himself. You don't have to go up to heaven – because the **Messiah** has already come down to you. You don't have to go down into the depths (Paul quotes the text in a slightly different way, in order to prepare for the interpretation he wants to give) – because the Messiah has already been raised from the dead. The strange, cryptic promises which spoke of the final undoing of the curse of exile have come true – in Jesus! He is God's fresh gift of grace, like the original law but in a completely new mode. This is Paul's own variation on the theme of Deuteronomy 30.

But why is Paul going to these lengths to say all this in what seems to us such a roundabout way? And how then does **faith**, 'calling on the name of the Lord', and salvation itself, fit into all this?

We must not forget, in reading this passage, that Paul is still addressing the question he raised at the start of the chapter. The desire of his heart is that his fellow Jews would be saved. But most of them have remained ignorant of God's covenant plan, fulfilled in Jesus the Messiah, the covenant plan through which the great promise of salvation in Deuteronomy 30 would come true. The answer to his own desire and prayer for the salvation of his fellow Israelites is threefold: (1) God has unveiled his salvation, a single way for all people as verses 11–13 make clear; (2) God has brought it near to them, as indeed to everybody, in a new way, for which different types of obedience to the original law become irrelevant; (3) all who openly acknowledge Jesus as Lord, and believe in their hearts that God raised him from the dead, are thereby wearing the badge which declares, in the present, that they are those whom God will save, vindicate and declare to be his people in the future.

This is where Paul's famous doctrine of '**justification** by faith' meets several of the other main themes in his thinking and writing. In order to make the connection between the **gospel** of Jesus and the promises of Deuteronomy, Paul quotes two other biblical texts: Isaiah 28.16 (already quoted in 9.33) in verse 11, and Joel 2.32 in verse 13. What counts as the badges in the present of those who will be saved, who will 'not be ashamed', in the future? First, 'believing in him'; second, 'calling upon the name of the Lord'. Verses 11, 12 and 13 thus explain verse 10, which in turn explains the crucial verse 9, which in turn makes the link with the quotation from Deuteronomy 30 in verse 8. If this sounds complex, it's because Paul has scampered through a fascinating train of thought, like a piece of music being played at speed. Let's slow it down a bit and listen more closely.

Deuteronomy speaks of God's 'word', the fresh act of God's saving grace, coming to be 'in your mouth and in your heart'. Paul glimpses the fact that this goes exactly with the two central things that happen to a person who has been grasped by the powerful gospel message (1.15–17; and see 1 Thessalonians 1.5 and 2.13), and who finds that their life has been transformed, turned inside out in the way that both Deuteronomy and Paul himself (2.29) describe as the 'circumcision of the heart'. Ordinary circumcision was the badge which marked out Jewish males. This transformed heart, visible in the public declaration of allegiance to Jesus as Lord and the belief that God had raised him from the dead, was the sign that someone was now a member of that renewed covenant family, the people promised by God in Deuteronomy 30.

Paul has, in other words, expounded an essentially Old Testament doctrine of salvation, composed his own variation on it, and shown that it has been fulfilled in Jesus the Messiah. Israel has been longing for salvation; God has provided it. You can see in the present time who is sharing in it, because they bear in their hearts and their mouths the only badges that count. But these badges, of course, are open to all, not only Jews. This is why, as Paul has insisted over and over throughout this letter, part of the point of the gospel is that non-Jews are welcome into this renewed covenant family on equal terms with Jews. If Jews want the salvation now provided in their own Messiah, they must (as Paul has learnt) share their Messiah, and the covenant family redefined in him, with a much larger company.

'Confessing Jesus as Lord' was what people did when getting baptized. This makes a link with Romans 6, but also reminds us of two other points, both of which are relevant to what Paul is saying here and throughout the letter. First, in Paul's world 'Lord' was a title for Caesar. Saying Jesus was 'Lord' meant, ultimately, that Caesar wasn't. Second, when Paul quotes from the prophet Joel in verse 13, 'Lord' in that passage refers of course to the 'Lord' of the Old Testament, YHWH, Israel's God. As in several other places, and here looking back to 9.5 in particular, Paul is quite clear that Jesus the Messiah, who died and rose again, was the personal embodiment of Israel's God, coming at last to do what he had always promised. In and through him, reversing the disaster of Israel's earlier failure (2.24), the name of Israel's God has now at last been glorified among the nations of the world.

ROMANS 10.14–21

The Call to the World, and the Failure of Israel

[14]So how are they to call on someone when they haven't believed in him? And how are they to believe if they don't hear? And how will they hear without someone announcing it to them? [15]And how will people make that announcement unless they are sent? As the Bible says, 'How beautiful are the feet of the ones who bring good news of good things.'

[16]But not all obeyed the good news. Isaiah asks, you see, 'Lord, who has believed our report?' [17]So faith comes from hearing, and hearing comes from the word of the Messiah.

[18]This might make us ask, did they not hear? But they certainly did:

Their sound went out into all the world,
and their words to the ends of the earth.

[19]But I ask, did Israel not know? To begin with, Moses says,

I will make you jealous with a non-nation;
and stir you to anger with a foolish people.

[20]Then Isaiah, greatly daring, puts it like this:

I was found by those who were not looking for me;
I became visible to those who were not asking for me.

[21]But in respect of Israel he says,

All day long I have stretched out my hands
to a disbelieving and disagreeable people.

Not long ago, some friends of ours came into possession of a large old house, and decided to do a first-class job of restoring it. To make sure all the details were taken care of, they hired a consultant to oversee all the bits and pieces, to advise them on colour, style and a thousand other things.

But from quite early on in the project, things started to go wrong. The consultant kept doing things our friends hadn't intended, and ignoring things they had specifically requested. The story was long and complicated, but I've said enough to give you the picture. What was going on was a clash between the actual stated intentions of the owners of the property and the ideas of the consultant – who, as became increasingly clear, was really trying to make the house look the way *he* would have wanted it.

When you meet a situation like that (this one, happily, was sorted out and everyone was content in the end) the only thing to do is to go back to the original plans and the owner's stated intentions. That's what Paul is doing in this passage. The problem he faces is that Israel has behaved like the consultant, trying to design God's people and God's plan the way they wanted instead of the way God wanted. Faced with this, Paul has a double task. Not only must he explain what God's original plan had been. He's now done that. He must also explain how even Israel's failure to believe was foreseen in Israel's scriptures themselves. He is like an advocate calling as a witness *against* the accused the very family and friends who might have been expected to speak up for him. By working through the different sections of Israel's own scriptures, and showing that God had always told Israel what he was up to, he makes it clear that the apparently strange design the owner had for the house – **Gentiles** flooding into God's people, many Israelites deliberately staying out – had been written into the blueprint all along.

This passage, then, picks up where the previous one left off, with the **good news** of salvation (Israel's own salvation, as in Deuteronomy 30!) being now thrown open to Gentiles as well as Jews. This might sound a very strange idea, yet Paul is determined to demonstrate that it's what God had in mind from the beginning, and that God had actually warned Israel that it is what would happen.

He begins with a chain of reasoning intended to show that he and his fellow **apostles**, in going to the Gentiles with the good news of Jesus, were not being disloyal to the traditions of Israel, but were actually fulfilling them. First he quotes from Isaiah 52.7, which is part of the build-up to the famous poem about the Suffering Servant of the Lord, which Paul and other early Christians saw as a prophecy of Jesus: how beautiful are the feet of the people who bring the good news, the **gospel**! It's a vivid metaphor, of course; neither the prophet nor Paul suppose that people are going to examine the actual feet of the messengers and award them a high score on some objective scale of beauty. The point is that the news is so good, so welcome, that those who receive it are like people who want to kiss the person delivering the mail for bringing them such a wonderful message. We can imagine someone, overjoyed with good news, feeling that even the wheels on the mail van were special because they had brought the vital letter. That's how Isaiah had prophesied that people would feel about the heralds as they ran to bring the good news of God's salvation to Israel. Paul has seen this again and again as he has gone around the Gentile world telling people that Jesus is Lord and that God raised him from the dead, and as this powerful gospel message has struck home to hearts and lives, bringing healing and salvation.

But now he faces a problem. Even in the Gentile world, plenty of people have heard this message and haven't believed it. Does this mean after all that he's making a mistake? No; this too was part of the strange prophetic script. He quotes from Isaiah 53.1, where the prophet is describing the Servant himself: 'Lord, who has believed what we were talking about?' Why some people believe and some don't is a mystery which Paul leaves in the hands of God alone. All he knows is that **faith** – the faith which in verses 8–13 was the key sign of human transformation – is what happens when people hear the message as it is announced, and that this message consists of the report about the **Messiah**. God's powerful **word** is at work whenever this report is given.

Could it be, though, that the Gentile nations have simply not heard the word? Is that why so many of them haven't as yet believed? Here, in verse 16, Paul surprises us by quoting from Psalm 19, a passage about God's hidden yet powerful message going out in all the created order, the message which (as in 1.18–20) all humans hear though not all heed. How Paul puts this revelation of God in all creation together with the more specific message of the gospel isn't clear, though it may be that he is thinking of something like what he says in Colossians 1.23, when the point seems to be that with the **resurrection** of Jesus a silent but powerful message ran like an earthquake through the whole created order, the message that corruption and death had been overthrown and new creation launched upon the world. Clearly Paul believed that the gospel message concerning Jesus was the fulfilment, not the overthrow, of the creator's plan for his creation and of his continuing close involvement with it. Thus the Gentile world does indeed know of its creator, and in principle at least of the rescue of creation through the gospel.

But this only makes it more poignant, more puzzling, that Israel itself has not believed the gospel. Having quoted Isaiah and the Psalms (representing two of the three main divisions of the Old Testament, the 'prophets' and the 'writings'), Paul now goes back to the '**law**', and once again to Deuteronomy in particular. Did Israel know, he asks, that God was about to do such a thing, revealing his salvation to pagan nations (the nations from whose rule Israel longed to be free!) while Israel itself remained in unbelief? Actually, yes, he concludes, Israel did know that he would do exactly this. In a passage soon after the one Paul has expounded in verses 5–8, God declares that he is going to make Israel 'jealous'. This will be a very important idea in the next chapter, and we must pay careful attention to what he means.

God made his basic promises of salvation to Israel; Israel clung on to them, often in the belief that they were for their nation and nobody else. But (as Paul has stressed over and over in this letter) the promises were intended to work *through* Israel for the benefit of the rest of the world. What will happen, then, when God acts through the Messiah to fulfil his original intention even though Israel itself clings to its own misinterpretation of the promises and, like the older brother in Jesus' **parable**, stays away from the party? Answer: Israel will be *jealous*, because (as Paul said in 9.30–31) Gentiles will be inheriting the promises while Israel, the promise-bearers, are missing out on them. The Gentiles are a 'non-people' in terms of the **covenant** (compare 9.26 and Ephesians 2.12), and they are 'foolish' because they lack the wisdom God has made available to Israel in the law (compare 2.19–20). But God will call precisely this people to arouse Israel to jealousy and anger. This sounds as though it will be simply bad news. But, as we shall see presently, Paul will use it as the lever to bring about the good news still to come.

Having anchored his basic point in the law itself, Paul returns to Isaiah to ram home the point, quoting two consecutive verses from the start of Isaiah 65. As he does so, we realize that he has come full circle from the point where he began in 9.30. What has in fact happened in and through the preaching of the gospel is the twofold shock: those who weren't even looking for salvation from Israel's God have stumbled into it, while those who were only too eager for it are missing out. Let's look at each of these in turn.

Gentiles had not been sitting around asking the kinds of questions to which Israel's traditions, and the gospel itself, were the answers. The gospel burst on them unawares, like someone announcing the end of a long and bitter war to people who hadn't even heard it was going on. The power of the message of the gospel itself had made the link between the salvation which fulfilled God's promises to Israel and the thoughts and aspirations of the Gentile people. They too belonged in the one creation of the one God, and what God had done for Israel had immediate implications for the whole world. Thus, like the extra guests in another of Jesus' parables, they found themselves enjoying a banquet they hadn't even known was being prepared.

Meanwhile Israel, the original invited guests, had made their lame excuses and shambled off about their own business. Indeed, as Paul discovered often enough during his work, not infrequently the very fact of Gentiles (oppressors and idolaters, as the Jews saw them) following Jesus made

Jewish people all the more determined not to believe the news that he was after all their own Messiah. How could he be, if all these unclean pagans were being allowed into his company without even getting **circumcised** to show that they were turning away from their idolatry and wicked practices?

This had been Paul's own position, of course, prior to his experience on the Damascus Road. But he saw it now as simply the fulfilment of yet another strange, haunting prophecy. Fancy being the chosen people of the one creator God, and yet turning your back when he came calling and stretching out his hands to offer you the very thing you'd been waiting for all along! Yet that is what Isaiah saw Israel doing: refusing to believe, and indeed contradicting God, disagreeing with his word – just as now, in Paul's experience, they were speaking against the new word of the gospel.

Of course the story doesn't stop there. Paul has set up the problem in its starkest terms, ready for the next chapter, in which he will tackle it from a fresh angle. But we do well to stop and ponder the strange path by which the gospel first made its way into the world, humbling the proud and lifting up the lowly. Is that what happens with the preaching of the gospel today? If not, why not?

ROMANS 11.1–6

The Remnant of Grace

¹So I ask, has God abandoned his people? Certainly not! I myself am an Israelite, from the seed of Abraham and the tribe of Benjamin. ²'God has not abandoned his people', the ones he chose in advance.

> Don't you know what the Bible says in the passage about Elijah, describing how he pleads with God against Israel? [3]'Lord,' he says, 'they have killed your prophets, they have thrown down your altars; I'm the only one left, and they are trying to kill me!' [4]But what is the reply from the divine word? 'I have left for myself seven thousand men who have not bowed the knee to Baal.'
>
> [5]In the same way, at the present time there is a remnant, chosen by grace. [6]But if it is by grace, it is no longer by works, otherwise grace would no longer be grace.

These days, we know quite a lot about depression. Many books are written about it, many different therapies are on offer for it, and it is no longer a taboo subject in the way it was not long ago.

The story of Elijah in 1 Kings 18 and 19 offers a text-book example of depression. He enjoys a huge triumph over the prophets of the pagan god Baal, calling down fire from **heaven** and having them all killed. It is a moment of elation, of high excitement. As a sign of that victory, the long drought that had blighted the land of Israel comes to an end. The rains are coming, he announces; and they do.

You might have thought this great victory would set him up for life, would leave him a happy man. But that's not how these things work, in human life or in the purposes of God. Queen Jezebel, herself a worshipper of Baal, is furious and puts out a warrant on his **life**. We feel all the energy going out of Elijah like the air out of a punctured bicycle tyre. He is terrified and runs away. He is lonely, hungry and exhausted: the classic conditions for serious depression. He sees everything – Israel, the world, himself and even God – through the distorting lens of his own low spirits.

His heart sinks into his boots, and all he wants to do is lie down and die. In fact, he asks God to take away his life. He's done his best, he says, and it's no good. The other side are still too powerful. He's the only one left; and now they're going to kill him.

It is highly significant that Paul chooses this story to help him launch the new stage of his argument at this key point in the letter. The previous two chapters might seem to have left him in a similar position to Elijah. He has worked and wept and prayed and taught and suffered to bring the **gospel** of Jesus the **Messiah** – Israel's Messiah! – to the wider world. This is designed to fulfil God's promises to the patriarchs, and to bring about the worldwide 'obedience of **faith**', the extension into the **Gentile** world of Israel's own call to be God's people. He has, in that sense, been like Elijah winning a great victory over the pagan world, not of course with the weapons of fire and sword but with the gospel-shaped weapons of love and suffering, truth and grace. And then he looks over his shoulder and sees his own countrymen, his beloved fellow Jews, in rebellion against this very gospel in which all their traditions are fulfilled, in which their own God has reached out in decisive and dramatic grace. In Romans 9 and 10 he has laid bare the story of God and Israel, seen from the vantage point of God's great act in Jesus the Messiah. But it has ended with Israel still being disobedient, still speaking against God's own **word** and deed. What hope can there be now?

This is not just a theological problem; it is a deeply personal one for Paul. He has spoken (9.1–3) of his constant sorrow and grief, of his own desire to be cut off from the Messiah if somehow that would help bring his fellow

Jews back to salvation (10.1). Left to himself, we can see how easy it would have been for him to sink into a depression similar to that of Elijah. Indeed, there are signs that at one point in his work that is exactly what happened (2 Corinthians 1.8–9). But, as in that passage, Paul allows the facts of the gospel to inform and re-mould his thinking and even his emotions. When you hit rock bottom, and perhaps only then, you are ready to hear the **message** of **resurrection**. That is what gives shape and energy to the solution he will now offer.

The question he faces in chapter 11 is quite simple: granted the apparent total failure of Israel to believe the gospel, as predicted by Moses and the prophets and as experienced in Paul's own work, does it appear that God has switched track and created a new people, formed from Gentiles rather than Jews? There have been (alas) many Christians who have believed something like that, who have reversed what they saw as the arrogance of Jewish privilege, and have regarded Jewish people as automatically *dis*barred from the church, and even from salvation. We who live with the memory of the Nazi wickedness, and of the long history of European anti-Semitism which created the climate for it, cannot look at such issues with calm detachment any more than Paul could.

But what is the answer? Have we not reached another point where, as in the argument of 3.1–8, God himself seems to have been painted into a corner? There it was the problem that God appeared to be caught between his obligation to keep his promises and his duty to bring justice to the world, including to sinful Israel. Now that problem has moved a stage further on. If God, faithful to his promises, has unveiled his plan of salvation fully and

43

finally in the Messiah, how can that faithfulness be worked out in practice in relation to the people to whom and through whom it was originally promised?

Paul does not answer this question all at once, but step by step. This passage is the first step. God, he says, has provided a *remnant*. It is an important biblical concept, and we must take a moment to walk round it and look at it from various angles.

The idea of a 'remnant', a few people who remain after a great disaster, comes from the heart of the Old Testament. Israel seems to have failed; great judgment falls; but there will be some survivors, a 'holy seed' (Isaiah 6.13) left like the stump of a felled tree, out of whose root new shoots may grow – an image which Paul develops later in the present chapter. 'A remnant shall return', declared the prophet (Isaiah 9.20–23, a passage Paul has already quoted in 9.27–28); in other words, after the **exile** in which Israel might have seemed to be banished for ever, a few people will be brought back again, and from that small beginning a renewed people will grow. Some Jewish groups of Paul's day, such as those who wrote the **Dead Sea Scrolls**, developed this idea, seeing themselves as the true 'remnant', the last Jews to remain faithful when everyone else had fallen away.

Paul has picked up this biblical idea and brought it forwards. What happened in the exile in Babylon (most Israelites exiled for ever, a few returning and starting again) is now happening to the Jewish people as they come through the greatest crisis of all, the work, death and resurrection of their Messiah. Most have refused to accept him, but some have done so. Paul himself is a good example: an Israelite, from Abraham's seed, and more specifically from the tribe of Benjamin, one of the two that remained in ancient Israel through all the catastrophes that came upon the rest. Paul is himself a sign that God has not finished with the Jewish people. Indeed, the passage he quotes in verse 2 ('God has not abandoned his people') comes from 1 Samuel 12.22, where the sign of God's faithfulness is the choice of Israel's first king, who happened to be called Saul, Paul's own Hebrew name.

But he isn't alone. There may be times when he feels like Elijah, but in fact (verse 5) there is a new 'remnant'. After all, all the early Christians were Jews. But Paul insists that this 'remnant' has a special character. It isn't like the 'remnant' in the Scrolls, consisting of a final few who are still faithful while all around have failed. Echoing 9.6–23 and various earlier passages in the letter, Paul stresses that the company of believing Jews, himself included, exist not because they deserved to, not because they formed a small number for whom keeping the **law** and clinging to ancestral privilege had worked after all, but because, once those props had been kicked away and they found themselves in the dock along with everyone else (3.19–20), God called them by sheer grace through the gospel. A glance ahead to verse 32 makes the point. Despite universal sin, God has found a way, through unmerited grace alone, to do once more, only now on a grander scale, what he did in the time of Elijah. There is, ultimately, no need to plunge into gloom over what seems to have happened. It is serious; but God's plans, God's power and God's grace are more than equal to the problem.

As we follow Paul's careful argument we would do well to reflect on ways in which, within our own lives and churches, the seemingly insuperable problems we confront constitute a call to us to reflect more deeply upon the sheer grace of God, and to pray more seriously for it to be poured out in a new way.

ROMANS 11.7–15

A Stumble with a Purpose

[7]What then? Did Israel not obtain what it was looking for? Well, the chosen ones obtained it – but the rest were hardened, [8]as the Bible says:

> God gave them a spirit of stupor,
> eyes that wouldn't see, and ears that wouldn't hear,
> right down to this present day.

[9]And David says,

> Let their table become a snare and a trap,
> and a stumbling-block and a punishment for them;
> [10]let their eyes be darkened so that they can't see,
> and make their backs bend low for ever.

[11]So I ask, then: Have they tripped up in such a way as to fall completely? Certainly not! Rather, by their trespass, salvation has come to the nations, in order to make them jealous. [12]If their trespass means riches for the world, and their impoverishment means riches for the nations, how much more will their fullness mean!

[13]Now I am speaking to you Gentiles. Insofar as I am the apostle of the Gentiles, I celebrate my particular ministry, [14]so that, if possible, I can make my 'flesh' jealous, and save some of them. [15]If their casting away, you see, means reconciliation for the world, what will their acceptance mean but life from the dead?

When Jesus told a story about an older and a younger brother, he was picking up echoes from several powerful stories in the book of Genesis. In Jesus' own **parable** in Luke 15, the younger son takes his share of the inheritance, goes off and wastes it all, and is then welcomed back lavishly by the father, which the older son resents with a bitter jealousy. The story ends without the family problem being resolved. Jesus seems to have wanted his hearers to think it through, to see where they belong within the story, and to act accordingly. But the echoes are all there. Cain is jealous of Abel because God accepts his offering (Genesis 4). Ishmael is rejected in favour of the younger Isaac (Genesis 21). Esau bitterly resents Jacob's trick in stealing his birthright and his blessing (Genesis 27). And then, on a grand scale, Joseph's older brothers, all ten of them, are furious that his father has favoured him. They think of killing him, but in the end they sell him into slavery (Genesis 37).

In each case, of course, the story includes God's vindication and establishment of the younger brother. In most cases the issue between the brothers is left unresolved: Abel is dead, Isaac and Ishmael live separate lives, Esau and Jacob negotiate a chilly truce. Only in the last instance is there any proper reconciliation. What Paul is doing in this passage, picking up the hint he had dropped at the end of the previous chapter, is telling a similar story but working it through to a fresh and positive conclusion. Israel as a whole is now in the position of the older brother; the **Gentile** Christians (joining the minority of Jews who have accepted the **gospel**) are in the position of the younger brother. This is bound to cause jealousy, as in all the background stories. But Paul has glimpsed that this jealousy

47

itself can become a motive which will propel at least some more Jews into **faith** and salvation. And he even dares to claim that this was the reason God allowed it to happen in the first place.

He will explain the deeper theological reasons for this in the next two passages. At the moment he is concerned to do two things. First, it is very important, in line with what he has said at the start of the chapter, to rule out any possibility of thinking that Israel might find a way to salvation by a route other than the faith spelled out in the previous chapter. For this reason, he draws once more on the closing chapters of Deuteronomy, this time 29.4, to show that in the **law** itself, at the very point where the terms of God's **covenant** with Israel were being established, Moses declares that Israel has remained blind and deaf to God's call and challenge – and that somehow God himself has been responsible for this. Here, we ought to remind ourselves, we are back in the strange but necessary territory we explored in chapter 9. The question we are bound to ask, and which Paul will answer as the present chapter continues, is: What is God up to? Why has he done this?

This question is heightened for us by the second quotation which Paul introduces, as so often balancing a passage from the law with another one from the Psalms (69.22–23). The connecting thought is the blindness that has afflicted most of Israel. **David**, speaking for God's true people, looks at the rest in rebellion against God, and declares that for those who go that way there can be no fresh light. Even their central symbolic act, the table-fellowship which expressed their solidarity as a nation, has become part of the problem instead of part of the answer. It has become a 'stumbling block', as in 9.33.

48

Once again we ask – as Paul must have asked a thousand times – What then is God up to? Why has he done this?

To answer the question, Paul develops both the theme of 'jealousy' we have already noted, and the idea of 'stumbling' which he has just reintroduced. Both come together in verse 11. Israel has tripped up, has stumbled over the stone which had been placed in its path. The word 'trespass' in verses 11 and 12 goes closely with this: it refers to the breaking of God's command, of course, but it carries also the sense of 'tripping up', of 'stepping on the wrong place and so losing your footing'. But all this, Paul says, was itself a necessary part of the process. Like Joseph explaining to his brothers that God had used their evil intent to bring about good (Genesis 50.20), Paul explains that the 'stumble' of Israel has been used, and even intended, by God in order to bring Gentiles flooding into the people of God, to the family of Abraham. Had Israel as a whole embraced the **Messiah**, he seems to be saying, it might have looked as though God's action in Jesus was reaffirming the special status of Israel, and leaving Gentiles as permanent second-class citizens. That was never the intention. God always wanted them to be members with equal standing, reflecting his universal sovereignty and rich mercy (10.12).

But this very move is the one which, Paul believes, was also designed to leave the unbelieving Jews in a position of 'jealousy'. Like the older brother in Jesus' story, they would look on and witness a small number of their own people (Paul included), and an increasingly large number of Gentiles, sharing and celebrating the blessings of the renewed **covenant**, the fulfilment of God's promise to Abraham. This is where we feel the full force of what Paul said in 9.4–5: these are *their* privileges – but the Gentiles are enjoying them! Why should they stay outside the party any longer? That is what Paul means in verses 13 and 14. He, a Jew, has been sent with a special commission to the Gentiles, as he explained in 10.14–18. But, as in 10.19, this had a second, hidden purpose. Not only was Paul's work supposed to be making the name and work of Israel's God known and loved in the non-Jewish world; it was also, by that very means, supposed to be making his fellow Jews 'jealous'. By that means, some of them at least might see that they were missing out on the fulfilment of their own heritage, and so come to faith and salvation.

We might suppose this was enough of a complex train of thought for one short passage, but there are two other things going on here which we cannot ignore.

First, in verse 14, Paul speaks of making 'my flesh' jealous (a point which most translations flatten out into 'my fellow Jews' or something like that). He is picking up what he said in 9.3: the people he is writing about are 'his kinsfolk according to the flesh'. Paul knows very well that 'flesh' is not the final reality, and that it can and does take people in the wrong direction. But that's part of the point, and should remind us of an earlier passage in the letter where we have heard something similar. In Romans 7, Paul writes with extraordinary power and passion of the way in which 'I, left to my own self' observe that 'my flesh' is in rebellion against God's true will. Now he writes with similar passion of how, 'left to my own self' (9.3), he has thought of praying that he himself might be cast away from God for the sake of 'his kinsfolk according to the flesh'. The strange drama of salvation, with all its tensions, is being played out in both cases, and in both cases Paul finds his own heart and mind caught up at the centre of it.

Second, what Paul says in verses 11 and 12 about Israel 'stumbling' and 'tripping up' looks back all the way to 5.20, where he declared that 'the law came in alongside, so that the trespass might be filled out to its full extent'. There, as we saw, the point was that Adam's sin, the sin of all humanity, was being acted out by Israel itself. Now at last we see how that strange idea is working itself out. When he speaks in verse 12 of Israel's 'failure' and 'impoverishment' bringing riches for the world and the nations; and when he speaks in verse 15 of their 'casting away' bringing reconciliation, and their 'acceptance' meaning '**life** from the dead', we catch our breath as we realize what he is proposing. He is asking us to imagine that what has happened to ethnic Israel in the purposes of God is nothing short of an acting out of what happened to the Messiah. He was brought low so that the world might be lifted up. He was cast away for the reconciliation of the world, and brought back to life so that all might live through him (4.24–25; 5.8–11). God has, as it were, written the story of the Messiah into larger history as the story of 'the Messiah's people according to the flesh' (9.5). The only way Paul knows how to understand what has happened to Israel is the pattern of Jesus the Messiah, the one in whom all God's secret wisdom is now revealed.

No wonder he looks at his unbelieving kinsfolk with sorrow and love. No wonder he looks at them with hope that some may still be saved. He sees in their rejection the face of the rejected Messiah, and in his glorious **resurrection** the possibility that they, too, may be welcomed back again. Let's give the story its proper conclusion, he seems to be saying. Let's settle this old jealousy once and for all. Once you learn to recognize God's hidden plan revealed in Jesus, all things are possible.

ROMANS 11.16–24

The Two Olive Trees

[16]Take another illustration: if the first fruits are holy, so is the whole lump.

And another: if the root is holy, so are the branches.

[17]But if some of the branches were broken off, and you – a *wild* olive tree! – were grafted in among them, and came to share in the root of the olive with its rich sap, [18]don't boast over the branches. If you do boast, remember this: it isn't you that supports the root, but the root that supports you.

[19]I know what you'll say next: 'Branches were broken off so that I could be grafted in.' [20]That's all very well. They were broken off because of unbelief – but you stand firm by faith. Don't get big ideas about it; instead, be afraid. [21]After all, if God didn't spare the natural branches, he certainly won't spare you.

[22]Note carefully, then, that God is both kind and severe. He is severe to those who have fallen, but he is kind to you, provided you continue in his kindness – otherwise you too will be cut off. [23]And they, too, if they do not remain in unbelief, will be grafted back in. God is able, you see, to graft them back in. [24]For if you were cut out of what is by nature a wild olive tree, and grafted, contrary to nature, into a cultivated olive tree, how much more will they, the natural branches, be grafted back into their own olive tree.

'This place isn't big enough for both of us!'

We've all heard it, or perhaps even said it. Sometimes it's in an office where two managers are both wanting their plans to go ahead. Sometimes it's in a sports team where two players both want to be the star. Sometimes, tragically, it's in a home where two squabbling teenagers both want to run things their way.

It's even uglier when this kind of rivalry gets played out in a church; and that's what Paul is anxious about here. He is still facing the question: granted that most Jewish people have rejected the **gospel** of the **Messiah**, does that mean God has written them off? Granted that some Jews, like himself, have formed a small number, a 'remnant chosen by grace' (verse 5), can any *more* Jews be saved, or is God now concentrating solely on non-Jews, on **Gentiles**?

Paul has just hinted in the previous passage that God does indeed intend to save more Jewish people, many more than had come to **faith** in Jesus at his time of writing. He now backs this up with two illustrations, the second of which develops into an entire story.

The first illustration, in verse 16, refers to the sacrificial system. When someone wanted to thank God for the harvest that was just beginning, they would bring the first portion of the produce (the 'first fruits') and offer them to God. By doing this they made the whole harvest 'holy', that is, dedicated to God. Very well, Paul declares: those Jews who at present have come to faith are like the 'first fruits', and that means that in principle the whole Jewish people have been presented to God. They cannot now be regarded as 'unholy' in the sense of being automatically outside God's people, unreachable by the gospel, unable to share in faith in Jesus.

Perhaps because this is essentially an agricultural picture, Paul's mind turns for a second illustration to the idea of a tree and its branches – specifically, an olive tree, one of the major sights and symbols of the Mediterranean world. One of the things everyone knew about olive trees was that, unless you cut them right down and uproot them, or perhaps burn them right through, they will live on and on, century after century. That is part of the point Paul is making.

But another thing most people would know about olive trees was that gardeners might from time to time perform a grafting operation. Some olives grew wild, and would often be quite strong in themselves though not producing good fruit. The gardener might decide to take that energy and harness it, by grafting shoots cut from a proper, cultivated olive into the trunk of the wild olive, thus combining the energy of the wild tree and the fruitfulness of the cultivated one. What Paul now wants to suggest is that when Gentiles become Christians the opposite is happening. They are like wild branches, grafted into the original cultivated olive tree.

Paul is well aware that this is against normal practice. Indeed (verse 24), he describes it as being 'against nature'. The reason he stresses this is to turn the situation around, and confront the Gentile Christians with the danger of arrogance. They are the ones who have been brought in by an extraordinary **miracle** of grace. They have no room, no right and no reason to boast over the original cultivated branches which have now, for the moment, been cut out of the tree.

Four things emerge very clearly from this. First, Paul is not backing down on what he has said in chapters 9 and 10. Those Jews who have not believed the gospel really are 'cut out of the tree'. That is why he has been so heartbroken over them (9.1–5), and so eager in prayer and hope to see them come back (10.1). But the way to come back has already been outlined in 10.5–13, and there is no other.

That is why he says here, in verse 23, that they can be grafted back 'if they do not remain in unbelief'. He is not for a moment suggesting, as many of his modern readers have wished he might, that the broken branches could be offered a way back which did not involve believing in Jesus as Messiah and Lord.

Second, Paul really does see the people of God as a single family, the children of Abraham now redefined around Jesus the Messiah and marked out by faith in him. This has been clear from at least chapter 4 onwards. The 'church' (though Paul doesn't use this word here) remains an essentially Jewish family into which non-Jews have been welcomed.

Third, Paul is insisting that just for this reason it makes good sense, and good theology, to believe that God can and will bring more Jews into this renewed family, which is after all their own true people. Insofar as it makes any sense to talk of things being easy or hard for God, Paul seems to be indicating in verse 24 that it's much easier for God to graft Jews back into the tree to which they belonged in the first place than to graft Gentiles in from the outside. God has done and is doing the harder thing, and the Gentile Christians in Rome are living proof of it. How much easier will it be for God to bring Jews back in as well.

Fourth – and this seems to be the real thrust of this passage – Paul is issuing a serious warning to the Gentile Christians. They must not suppose for a moment that they have 'replaced' Jews in God's plan, that the church is now a 'Gentiles-only' family, or (worse) that God has chosen them precisely *because* they are Gentiles. That would be to make the same mistake in reverse as the Jews had made earlier, namely, to imagine that God's grace was tied to a

particular ethnic group. And if they make that mistake –
relying on ethnic identity as the badge of membership in
God's people, instead of faith alone – they can expect God
to react the same way he had done with unbelieving Israel.
There are no promises of salvation for those who think it's
their birthright.

Why would Paul need to issue this solemn warning? Did
he know that the Gentile Christians in Rome were already
beginning to think this way? We can't be sure. But we do
know that, around the time he was writing this letter,
a large number of Jews were allowed back to Rome after
having been banished a few years earlier. And we do know
that many ordinary people in Rome distrusted and disliked
the Jews and sneered at them. How easy it would have been,
in those circumstances, for the little church in Rome, mostly
composed of Gentile Christians, to pick up the attitude
of society all around and join in the general anti-Judaism
of the day. How easy it would be to say to their contemporaries that they had embraced a new religion, which began
admittedly in Judaism but now had happily become a
different sort of thing altogether. (Roman society was
always open to new kinds of religion!) That, says Paul,
would be a fatal mistake, showing that they were losing
their grip on the gospel itself.

In particular, it would show that they were losing their
grip on God himself. How easy it is for us, too, to forget
one aspect or another of who God is. Verse 22 is one of
many lessons in understanding God that this letter has to
offer. Some people imagine God to be always severe, always
cross, always ready to find fault. Such people urgently need to
discover just how kind and gracious God has been in Jesus
the Messiah, and how this grace is theirs for the asking. But

other people sometimes imagine that God is simply kind and generous in a sense which would rule out his ever rebuking or warning anyone about anything. Such people urgently need to discover just how much God hates evil in all its destructive and damaging ways, and how firmly he confronts, and ultimately rejects, those who persist in perpetrating it. The Roman Christians needed to learn this double lesson in the very first Christian generation. Many Christians and churches still need to learn it today.

ROMANS 11.25–32

Mercy Upon All

[25]My dear brothers and sisters, you mustn't get the wrong idea and think too much of yourselves. That is why I don't want you to remain in ignorance of this mystery: a hardening has come for a time upon Israel, until the fullness of the nations comes in. [26]That is how 'all Israel shall be saved', as the Bible says:

> The Deliverer will come from Sion,
> and will turn away ungodliness from Jacob.
> [27]And this will be my covenant with them,
> Whenever I take away their sins.

[28]As regards the good news, they are enemies – for your sake! But as regards God's choice they are beloved because of the patriarchs. [29]God's gifts and God's call, you see, cannot be undone. [30]For just as *you* were once disobedient to God, but now have received mercy through *their* disobedience, [31]so *they* have now disbelieved as well, in order that, through the mercy which has come *your* way, they too may now receive mercy. [32]For God has shut up all people in disobedience, so that he may have mercy upon all.

I have only once knowingly met a man who had committed murder.

He grew up in the deep South of the United States, and learned from an early age to hate all black people and to believe that they were part of a great conspiracy to take over the world and ruin everything that the USA stood for. His heart – as he later came to describe it – was filled with hatred and anger, and he was ready to do anything to fight for his vision of what should happen. One day the opportunity came, and he took it . . .

Some while later, while serving his prison sentence, he began to read the Bible. All sorts of things happened to him, deep down inside, and God's grace healed him and enabled him to repent and reject the entire package of lies he had believed, and with it to get rid of all the hatred and anger. He was eventually released, and has devoted his life ever since to working for the Christian **gospel**, not least to bring about reconciliation between black and white people.

As part of this project, he has written a book in which he has told his story. It is called *He's My Brother*. In it, he and a new-found friend, a black man, explain how they had completely overcome the prejudice which had formerly kept them apart. The word in the title says it all. Formerly he could never have dreamed of calling a black man 'brother'. Now it was the most natural and appropriate thing in the world.

We should never miss the significance of Paul's little words. He has been emphasizing his sorrow and tears over 'his brothers, his kinsfolk according to the flesh' (9.3). He has had stern words for **Gentile** Christians: they must not think that they have displaced Jews in God's favour and set up a new system of inverted privilege. How easy it would be now for his readers to think, 'Oh, so Paul is simply treating us as second-class citizens after all; he's saying that Jews like him are the real insiders in God's people, and we simply get in on his coat-tails.' This of course is not at all what Paul is thinking or saying, but it's desperately easy for people to get the wrong end of the stick. So Paul begins his final summing-up of the long argument of chapters 9—11 with the little word that says it all: *adelphoi*, 'brothers' (which in his world included 'sisters' as well). Paul has lived and worked and prayed and struggled for the full and equal rights of Gentile Christians, and he wants them to be quite clear that he has not gone back on that for a split second. His fellow Jews are his 'brothers according to the flesh', but Gentile Christians and Jewish Christians alike are, in a full and complete sense, his true family, fellow members of the body of the **Messiah**.

This launches him into stating, and then explaining, the 'mystery' which explains the whole picture. The word 'mystery' was every bit as exciting to ancient readers as it is to us, and in Paul's world it had a particular meaning: the secret plan of God, which was now unveiled in the Messiah, Jesus. (This isn't, as some people have suggested, a *fresh* 'mystery', quite apart from the Messiah, which God has only now revealed to Paul.) The 'mystery' is the question: how is God saving his whole people, Jew and Gentile alike? How is 'all Israel' going to be saved (verse 26)?

Many people find this puzzling. Surely, they say, 'all Israel' must mean 'all Jews' – either all Jews who have ever lived, or all believing Jews, or all Jews alive at the time of final salvation. But Paul himself has indicated otherwise. At the very start of the discussion, in the passage beginning at 9.6, he has declared that 'not all who are of Israel are in fact of Israel'. In a similar passage in Galatians (6.16), he has spoken of the 'Israel of God', meaning the whole family of the Messiah, Jew and Gentile alike (compare Galatians 3.26–29). Some translations of Romans, assuming that verse 26 refers to all *Jews* being saved, make it sound as though Paul here refers to a fresh event which comes *after* the events at the end of verse 25, but that's not what Paul says. 'A hardening has come upon Israel, allowing time for the nations to come in; *and that is how* God is saving "all Israel".' The phrase 'all Israel shall be saved' was already something of a regular slogan in some Jewish thinking; Paul here takes it and widens its scope. All Israel? That means all the family of Abraham – and that includes believing Gentiles as well as believing Jews (4.16).

What then is this 'hardening', and how does it work? As in 2.1–16 and 9.6–29, both of which repay careful study when reading the present passage, Paul has in mind the strange divine action whereby, when someone rebels against God's will, God allows that person to continue in rebellion rather than judging them at once. God stays his hand and creates a space of time in which other things can happen; and, with God, the 'other things' are always the spread of blessing into the wider world. The point of Israel's 'hardening' – of the process whereby most Jews have refused to believe the gospel, and the fact that this too seems to be part of God's strange purpose – has been in order to allow time for the non-Jewish nations to come in on equal terms.

This is more or less exactly what Paul had said in 11.11–12 and 11.15. (This shows again, incidentally, that Paul is not here adding a new point to the argument, but continuing to explore and then summarize the one he has already been making.) If ethnic Israel had embraced the gospel from the very start, it would have been fatally easy for them to assume that they had always been entitled to it, and that if any Gentiles came in they would rank below them. This would mean, in the language of 11.6, that grace would no longer be grace. But Paul has insisted all along that all humans, Jews as well as Gentiles, are sinful (3.19–20; 3.23), and that all who come into God's family must do so on the basis of sheer grace and mercy alone. What we are seeing in the present passage is in fact Paul's final resolution of the problem which is bound to occur when God decides to act for the salvation of the world through a people who are themselves part of the problem as well as the bearers of the solution. It had to be like this; only so could the creator God be true to his creation, the **covenant** God be true to the covenant. This is the way in which God is 'righteous' or 'just'.

That is why, when Paul quotes from the Bible to back up his point, he carefully chooses a combination of passages which make just this point. Taken together, Isaiah 59.20, Jeremiah 31.33–34 and Isaiah 27.9 speak, not of special privilege coming to Israel aside from the Gentiles, but of God working for the benefit of Gentiles through the fulfilment of the covenant with Israel (the Deliverer will come *from* Sion, out into the wider world), and of God re-affirming that covenant itself not by pretending that all Jews do after all have a private path to salvation irrespective of the fact that they are sinners just like the Gentiles, but by declaring that, in the course of his continuing work in the world, he will also 'turn away ungodliness from Jacob' and 'take away their sins'. That last passage comes from Jeremiah 31, where the prophet speaks not of the original covenant but of the new, renewed covenant in which, after the terrible **exile** which formed God's judgment on their sin, Israel would at last be welcomed back again. This is the same point that Paul was picking up in 10.5–13 by working through Deuteronomy 30.

So he sums up the picture in a few short sentences. Unbelieving Jews are at present 'enemies', opposing the gospel and so, paradoxically, continuing to create that breathing space in which Gentiles can come in. But they remain 'beloved' in the sense that God continues to yearn over them, as a father for a long-lost son. That original relationship can never be taken away or denied (verse 29). And, because of it, Gentile Christians urgently need to learn the lesson of verses 30 and 31. This is the sequence. First, the Gentiles were disobedient. Then the Jewish people as a whole rejected the gospel – and that created a space for the Gentiles to come in. Now, however, with Gentiles receiving mercy, the Jewish people will, Paul believes, become 'jealous' of them (verse 14) and so turn away from unbelief (verse 23) and find mercy. This will happen, not just at some future date, but 'now', in the present time, as he says at the end of verse 31.

Like everything else in Romans, all this depends ultimately on something about God. This is how God has decided to act to rescue a world characterized by disobedience through and through. If he was to work within the world to save the world – and, having made a good world, that was the only appropriate way to work – that would necessarily involve him in choosing and calling some of his creatures, themselves sinful, to work through, creating the context for his own coming on the stage of human history in the person of the Messiah to bear the sin of the world.

(The death and **resurrection** of Jesus, though seldom mentioned in chapters 9—11, is after all present underneath, determining the shape of the thought and argument.) But in order for the mercy thereby gained to be available for all as a gift of grace rather than a privilege or right, it was necessary for all people, Jew as well as Gentile, to be shut up in the prison called 'disobedience'. Only so could grace be grace, with all human pride being humbled, and mercy – as opposed to reward – made available for all. That is the big picture of the plan of God which Paul has finally laid before us.

Whenever I try to explain this, someone asks (and if they didn't I would have to ask it myself): isn't that all very complex and tortuous? Couldn't there have been a simpler, and perhaps a better, way? I suspect that Paul's answer would have been to take us back to several of the earlier stages in the letter, in particular to chapter 3. What would we have preferred God to do? Can we solve, better than he has done, the dilemmas of a good creation, universal sin and unbreakable covenant promises? Could there have been another way, other than the incarnation, death and resurrection of Jesus, Israel's Messiah according to the flesh and also 'God over all, blessed for ever' (9.5)?

ROMANS 11.33–36

To God Be the Glory

> [33]O, the depth of the riches
> And the wisdom and knowledge of God!
> We cannot search his judgments,
> We cannot fathom his ways.
> [34]For 'who has known the mind of the Lord?

63

> Or who has given him counsel?
> [35]Who has given a gift to him
> Which needs to be repaid?'
> [36]For from him, through him and to him are all things.
> Glory to him for ever! Amen.

I was taken yesterday to see the site of a new bridge across a river.

We parked the car in a grassy wood and set off to walk. The trees were quite thick to begin with, and I couldn't see the river, though I could hear it. I assumed the bridge was to be an ordinary one, connecting two banks not far apart, at a height of maybe fifteen or twenty feet above the water.

Suddenly, as the trees thinned out, I looked from side to side and realized to my alarm that we were on a ledge jutting out with sheer sides and a long drop. There was a wall ahead of us, preventing us seeing where we were going. We carefully squeezed round the edge of the wall and found ourselves on a ledge, looking down a hundred feet and more to the swirling river below. This was where an old railway bridge had crossed the river, thirty years ago, on a huge viaduct. Only the stone pillars at either side remained. The plan, so my guides explained, was to reconnect the two sides with a suspension footbridge. It would be spectacular, breathtaking.

I couldn't go too near the edge. I am all right with heights up to a point, but there was no fence, and a strong wind was blowing. I was filled with admiration for the daring, the simplicity and the skill both of the plan and of how the finished product would look.

That is how Paul expects us to feel as we come round the last bend in this, his greatest piece of writing. We may not have expected to emerge at this point with this view. We are certainly liable to find ourselves suffering from theological vertigo, if not sheer terror, as well as intellectual exhaustion. But there is a wonderful simplicity about the argument, or rather about the plan of God as Paul has laid it out. It looks dangerous, and indeed, in one sense, it is; it is always possible for people to take this bit or that bit of what he says and construct a scheme of their own which doesn't quite manage to keep its balance the way Paul has done. No doubt some may think my own treatment is guilty of this too, and that may well be the case. But this is the point in the argument when the only thing left to do is to take a long, deep breath and shake our heads in wonderment, and give praise to the God whose thoughts, plans and accomplishments are so much deeper and greater than anything we could have imagined for ourselves.

When Jewish people want to praise God, they have a rich tradition to draw on in the Bible, and Paul draws together several passages to heap up not only praise itself but the echoes of Israel's praise down the ages. The Psalms are full of declarations of how extraordinary God is in his wisdom and love. Proverbs and Job celebrate that sense of wonder and mystery at the way in which God is always out ahead of us, ready to surprise us by doing new things which none the less, in retrospect, are exactly right and full of rich wisdom and insight far beyond anything we could have fathomed. Passages like Job 5.9, 15.8 and 36.22 and 23 echo underneath verses 33 and 34; verse 35 then quotes directly from Job 41.11, near the conclusion of that great book. God is never in anyone's debt. It is a perpetual human failing to imagine that he is – to suppose that we can establish a claim on God either by our birth, our beauty, our brains or our behaviour. But we can't. Nobody is ever in the position of giving God a gift which demands repayment while they sit back smugly, knowing they are in the right and waiting for God to get his act together.

In fact, as the final verse indicates in a triumphant sweep of thought, everything we are comes from him. Everything we have comes from him. Everything that exists, the whole of creation, is his handiwork and is sustained in existence by his power and love. Everything we do traces itself back into his presence as the sovereign one before whom all human work and activity is, at best, loving service.

This kind of all-embracing statement of God's universal sovereignty is always in danger of ignoring the obvious problems. The world as we see it, and humans as we see and know them – including of course our own selves – show plenty of signs that all is still not well. Many have said in our own day, as they said in Paul's, that if the world as we presently experience it is all directly traceable to a single God then, to put it mildly, it looks as though God has good days and bad days, as though some parts of his world are very good while others are a bit less than that or perhaps downright bad. But Paul has dealt throughout this letter with just these problems. Romans as a whole has been about the saving, restorative justice of God. It has taken on board the fact not only of universal human idolatry, disobedience and sin but also the corruption to which all creation has been subjected as a result (8.18–27). This letter, above all other writings in early Christianity, wrestles with exactly these problems in the light of the death and **resurrection** of Jesus the **Messiah** and the gift of the **spirit**, and demonstrates that God has been true both to creation and to **covenant**, and that this faithfulness will work its way out – is already working its way out – to the point where we can see the end from the beginning.

The project of God's new creation, like the proposed bridge over the river we were imagining, is not yet complete. But the architect has designed it. The foundations are securely laid. The work is already well in hand. The final completion is not in doubt. It is time to stand back, not exactly in admiration – that implies a kind of cool appraisal, an approving nod from one who might in principle have done such a thing themselves – but in sheer awe and breathtaking wonder at the scale and scope of it all. Glory to God for ever! Amen.

ROMANS 12.1–5

The Living Sacrifice

[1]So, my dear family, this is my appeal to you by the mercies of God: offer your bodies as a living sacrifice, holy and pleasing to God. This is your true and appropriate worship. [2]What's more, don't let yourselves be squeezed into the shape dictated by the present age. Instead, be transformed by the renewing of your minds, so that you can work out what God's will is, what is good, acceptable and complete.

[3]Through the grace which was given to me, I have this to say to each one of you: don't think of yourselves more highly than you ought to think. Rather, think soberly, in line with faith, the true standard which God has marked out for each of you. [4]As in one body we have many limbs and organs, you see, but none of the parts of the body have the same function, [5]so we, many as we are, are one body in the Messiah, and individually we belong to one another.

William was coming to the end of his first year as chairman of the company when I met him at a lunch.

'How's it been going?' I asked.

'Oh,' he said, 'it's been wonderful in several ways. The company is doing well and I'm proud to be part of it.'

'Why only several ways?' I asked, picking up the implied hesitation in the way he had answered.

'Well,' he said, 'I've only just realized what my problem has been. Everybody in the company has a clear idea of how they want the chairman to act, what sort of meetings they think they need, and so on. I've done my best to make my number with everyone. I've gone out of my way to learn the procedures they have in place. But I've figured out now that I've gone too far. I've let their expectations dictate the shape of my work, of how I spend my time. I now need to turn that inside out. I have my own ideas of what we should be doing, and from now on I'm going to set the pace.'

Now, of course, a wise executive will want to listen carefully to those who know more about the company than he or she does. To this extent the picture doesn't quite fit what Paul is saying. But it does in the all-important point: his appeal now is that we should refuse to let 'the **present age**' squeeze us into its mould, dictate to us how we should think and indeed *what* we should think, and tell us how we can and can't behave. Instead, we are to be transformed; our minds need to be renewed. We have to set the pace ourselves, and work out what sort of people we should be. The basis for this is not what the surrounding culture expects of us, but what God in his mercy has done for us.

One of the key phrases here is 'the present age' (verse 2). In Galatians 1.4 Paul calls this 'the present *evil* age'. Like many first-century Jews, he believed that world history was divided into 'the present age', characterized by rebellion against God and the corruption and death which result, and 'the **age to come**', in which God would give new **life** to the world and humankind, bringing justice, joy and peace once and for all. Part of the point of Paul's **gospel** is his belief that this 'age to come' had already begun in Jesus, and supremely in his death and **resurrection**.

Christians are therefore in the position, not (to be sure) of a new executive learning the job, but of someone who needs to stop letting the world around dictate its own terms and conditions, and who instead must figure out how to think, speak and act as is appropriate not for the present age but for the new age which is already breaking in. Christians are called to be counter-cultural – not in all respects, as though every single aspect of human society and culture were automatically and completely bad, but at least in being prepared to think through each aspect of life. We must be ready to challenge those parts where the present age shouts, or perhaps whispers seductively, that it would be easier and better to do things *that* way, while the age to come, already begun in Jesus, insists that belonging to the new creation means that we must live *this* way instead.

The key to it all is the transforming of the *mind*. Many Christians in today's world never come to terms with this. They hope they will be able to live up to something like Christian standards while still thinking the way the rest of the world thinks. It can't be done. Paul's analysis of human rebellion against God in 1.18–32 included a fair amount of wrong *thinking*. Having the mind renewed by the persuasion of the **spirit** is the vital start of that true human living which is God's loving will for all his children.

This, after all, is a way of growing up to maturity. People sometimes suggest that living a Christian life means a kind of immaturity, since you are guided not by thinking things through for yourself but by rules and regulations derived from elsewhere. That isn't Paul's vision of Christian living. Of course there are plenty of firm boundaries. He will have more to say about them presently. But at the centre of genuine Christianity is a mind awake, alert, not content to take a few guidelines off the peg but determined to understand *why* human life is meant to be lived in one way rather than another. In fact, it is the way of life of 'the present age' which often involves the real human immaturity, as people simply look at the surrounding culture, with all its shallow and silly patterns of behaviour, and copy it unthinkingly.

For Paul, the mind and the body are closely interconnected, and must work as a coherent team. Having one's mind renewed and offering God one's body (verse 1) are all part of the same complete event. Here Paul uses a vivid, indeed shocking, idea: one's whole self (that's what Paul means by 'body') must be laid on the altar like a **sacrifice** in the **Temple**. The big difference is that, whereas the sacrifice is there to be killed, the Christian's self-offering is actually all about coming alive with the new life that bursts out in unexpected ways once the evil deeds of the self are put to death. (To get the full picture, we need to see the several ways in which this passage stands on the shoulders of others like 6.1–14 and 8.12–17.) Christian living never begins with a set of rules, though it contains them as it goes forwards. It begins in the glad self-offering of one's whole self to the God whose mercy has come all the way to meet us in our rebellion, sin and death. Within that, it involves the renewal of the mind so that we are enabled both to think straight, instead of the twisted thinking that the world would force upon us, and to act accordingly.

One of the first things that Christians need to get their minds around – and one of the things that will have an immediate impact on the way we live – is the call to live as different members of a single family. Paul has already warned the Roman Christians against thinking too highly of themselves (11.25). Being loved unconditionally by the creator God makes you quite special enough without imagining that your family membership or civic background can make you any more so! Now he warns them again that they are to regard themselves, not as the 'premier-league' Christians while people in other places or from other backgrounds are in a kind of second rank, but as simply various limbs and organs of the one body which also possesses many others.

This is one of two famous passages (the other one being 1 Corinthians 12) in which Paul uses this image of the body with its limbs and organs in order to stress that the church is a unity made up of quite different members. 'One body in the **Messiah**'; that is the way he puts it here, in verse 5. The Messiah is the truly human being, as well as being 'God over all' (9.5); those who are 'in him', members of his 'body', form God's renewed humanity. In other words, the picture of 'body and members' isn't simply an illustration at random. It is designed to speak of the new human life which the church is to live and model before the world.

This is one of those points where we begin to detect something of Paul's wider purpose for the church, which will become more and more apparent as the next chapters go on. People sometimes suppose that the 'theological' part of Romans is finished with chapter 11, and that what we have from here on is simply 'practical' teaching. Paul is seldom as unsubtle as that. (In any case, there has been a lot of 'practical' or 'ethical' teaching already in the letter, as we have seen in chapters 6 and 8.) Rather, the appeal for church unity, which will be spelled out in more detail in chapters 14 and 15, grows directly out of everything Paul has been saying throughout the letter about the coming together of Jew and **Gentile** in the Messiah.

That unity is not simply based on a general belief that everyone matters. It is based, as we saw in chapters 3 and 4 (and in Galatians 2, 3 and 4), on the fact that Christians all have the same **faith**. God has given each Christian the same faith in Jesus as the risen Messiah and Lord. However different people may be, in temperament, background, calling and ability, all Christians share this faith, and it is the ground of their unity and co-operation.

This is a lesson the church of our own day needs to learn afresh. The world around us loves to force us into disunity. We must once more be transformed by having our minds renewed, not least through the self-offering of worship. That way, as we learn the lessons of unity, we may perhaps discover how to put them into effect.

ROMANS 12.6–13

Living Together in the Messiah

[6]Well then, we have gifts that differ in accordance with the grace that has been given to us, and we must use them appropriately. If it is prophecy, we must prophesy according to the pattern of the faith. [7]If it is serving, we must work at

our serving; if teaching, at our teaching; [8]if exhortation, at our exhortation; if giving, with generosity; if leading, with energy; if doing acts of kindness, with cheerfulness.

[9]Love must be real. Hate what is evil, stick fast to what is good. [10]Be truly affectionate in showing love for one another; compete with each other in giving mutual respect. [11]Don't get tired of working hard. Be on fire with the spirit. Work as slaves for the Lord. [12]Celebrate your hope; be patient in suffering; give constant energy to prayer; [13]contribute to the needs of God's people; make sure you are hospitable to strangers.

The seven friends met, as they had arranged, at ten o'clock the next morning. It had been a late night. They had all been excited. Now they were a little apprehensive at how they were going to take the project forward.

They had discovered that they were all interested in gardens, interested to the point of being ready to give up the various jobs they had at present and work together at a new business. There wasn't a proper garden centre for twenty miles in either direction; there was clearly a hole in the market; the question was, how were they going to get started? Who was going to do what?

Geoffrey and Ruth were the natural leaders. The rest quickly agreed that they should co-ordinate the whole project. Geoffrey had all kinds of contacts in the business world, both in their area and in London. He could talk through strategy with people who would give them good advice, and he would keep a sharp eye on the larger scene. Ruth had worked in the bank for twenty years, and would be the obvious choice to run the financial side of the business. Meanwhile Thomas, who could never look after his own money never mind anybody else's, was itching to start growing things, especially vegetables, and was delighted when the rest of the group agreed that he should look after that section. Rebecca, who had been a keen gardener since she was a little girl, would look after the flowers and shrubs. Gerry was one of nature's handymen; give him a few minutes, and he could put up a fence, fix a lawnmower, make a display cabinet or repair a broken wheelbarrow. They were going to need him all right. Matthew knew the county like the back of his hand, and in a previous job had learnt the art of encouraging people to buy things they hadn't originally known they wanted. He would get out on the road and find new business.

And Richard? There was an awkward pause. What could he do? He wasn't particularly good with his hands, though he loved gardens and was just as keen on the business as the rest of them. He had an academic background but didn't want to pursue it. But he was everyone's best friend in the group, the one who made them all cheerful. Suddenly they realized. He would be the key person in the main office, greet people as they came in, organize all the paperwork and the files, and write up reports. He would keep them all happy – and the customers as well. The business was launched.

If only it could be like that in the church, I can hear many Christians thinking. But it should be! God gives different people different gifts that are needed for the work of the **gospel** to flourish. This is partly a matter of what we call 'natural temperament'; some people are natural leaders, some are born teachers, others are naturally open, generous-hearted people. But it's also a matter of grace, as Paul says in verse 6. God's grace often enhances the abilities and inclinations people already have; but sometimes, when

God's **spirit** takes over someone's life, new gifts emerge that neither they nor anyone else imagined before.

It is vital that the church should recognize and value these different gifts – and that those to whom they have been given should place them in the service of the church, as part of the sacrificial self-offering spoken of at the start of the chapter. Here we run into a problem. It isn't always nearly as easy as in the illustration. Sometimes there are people who (so to speak) are absolutely determined that they should be running the vegetable section when everyone else knows perfectly well they would be a disaster at it and are much better out on the road selling to new customers. Sometimes people speak of 'my ministry' in the tone of voice which says that, whether or not the rest of the church wants to recognize it, God has given them a particular task and the church has a responsibility to provide them with an opportunity to fulfil it whether it makes any sense or not. Equally, it often happens that a particular church, for whatever reason, remains blind and deaf to what God is saying in and through particular people, and never benefits from the grace that God wants to pour out through them.

Having said all that, it is wonderful to see the ways in which God does indeed provide different graces and gifts, and the church does indeed benefit. Verses 6 to 8 list some of them, and we should note that there is no sense that some or all of them come with the label 'ordination' on them. Prophecy – the spirit-led interpretation of scriptural truth – may be given to anyone, though those who sense that God wants them to speak out on particular issues have a responsibility not to say the first thing they think the spirit is prompting them to say (that way lie all kinds of dangers) but to regulate it 'according to the pattern of the **faith**'. If, in other words and just as an example, you're talking about Jesus, you should be clear what the Christian faith teaches about him and not contradict it. Exercising gifts is never a matter simply of letting 'inspiration' take over. That would be to capitulate to one particular cultural mood (the 'Romantic' movement in particular) rather than to grow up as mature Christians.

Most of the tasks in verses 7 and 8, in fact, involve hard work, and Paul encourages his readers to get ready for it. The passage has a 'get-your-sleeves-rolled-up' feel to it. Find out what your task is and give yourself to it properly: plan the work, think it through, get up early and get on with it. Expect to work till you're tired, and to keep at it even on the days when you're not in the mood. You can't just play at it when you 'feel like it'. Christian service isn't a hobby, though people sometimes think of it like that; it's a divine calling, and if that calling is to make cups of coffee after church, that needs to be done with energy, care and flair (and, I hope, using coffee that's been produced according to Christian standards of justice and fair trading). People with a gift of teaching shouldn't just expect to be able to stand up and say whatever they think at the time; they should think it through, prepare their material, always be working at filling in gaps, seeing a larger picture, and at being able to communicate it better. And so on. Note, in particular, the command to cheerfulness when doing acts of kindness. Nothing undermines Christian work so instantly as a gloomy face.

Or, for that matter, a false smile. The word for 'genuine' in verse 9 means, literally, 'unhypocritical'. This poses a problem for many people today. If I really don't like someone, they say, how can I love them? But if I'm commanded to love them, and try to act as if I do, doesn't that make me a hypocrite?

Part at least of the answer is that, for Paul, 'love' is more about what people do than about how they feel. In fact, in the early church 'love' was often connected quite directly to helping other people out in their various needs, not least financial, rather than necessarily to having warm feelings towards them. As a Christian, it is possible, not least through prayer, to decide firmly that one is going to help someone in need, whether or not you particularly like them.

Of course that can be done coldly and patronizingly. But again and again in Christian experience we discover that when we behave towards someone *as though we really did love them*, then, to our surprise, love, care and concern for the other person's welfare quickly spring up. We do well to remind ourselves that if we waited until we were quite sure our motives were completely pure and right we might never actually get around to doing anything at all.

The commands in verses 9 to 13, unlike the specific tasks listed in verses 6, 7 and 8, are meant for all Christians. Of course some will need, more than others, the command to be patient in suffering. Some, more than others, will be in a position to exercise generous hospitality. But all Christians should expect to do all of these most of the time. Read through these verses again and again and feel the simple, practical energy they evoke. They offer a no-nonsense vision of Christian living. In particular, we should note the remarkable command in verse 9: hate what is evil, stick fast to what is good. You can't get simpler, or clearer, than that. Paul assumes that everybody knows, up to a point at least, that there are a great many things that are evil and a great many that are good. Christians need to be reminded that they are not exempt from following the basic human moral standards that almost all societies recognize. Indeed, as the next passage will indicate, they are to be in the forefront of showing the rest of the world what a genuine human life looks like.

ROMANS 12.14–21

Living Alongside the World

[14]Bless those who persecute you; bless them, don't curse them. [15]Celebrate with those who are celebrating, mourn with the mourners. [16]Come to the same mind with one another. Don't give yourselves airs, but associate with the humble. Don't get too clever for yourselves.

[17]Never repay anyone evil for evil; think through what will seem good to everyone who is watching. [18]If it's possible, as far as you can, live at peace with all people. [19]Don't take revenge, my dear people, but allow God's anger room to work. The Bible says, after all, 'Vengeance is mine; I will repay, says the Lord.' [20]No: 'If your enemy is hungry, feed him; if he is thirsty, give him a drink. If you do this, you will pile up burning coals on his head.' [21]Don't let evil conquer you. Rather, conquer evil with good.

The headline said one word, in thick black letters right across the top of the front page: REVENGE.

The story was a classic tale of spurned love. A woman whose husband had cheated her and gone off with her best friend had bided her time, waited for her opportunity and then killed them both, not instantly but in a way which allowed her to extract maximum satisfaction by giving them maximum terror.

A nasty, sorry, sordid story of course. But the reason it made the front page was, I suspect, that deep down a lot of us know someone we would like, as we say, to 'get even with'. Someone has done something to us which we have allowed to fester. If we had the courage, or the folly, we would love to get our own back. More worrying still, at any given moment there is probably someone who would love to take revenge on us. The desire for revenge is like a deep itch somewhere right down inside. The newspapers know that if we can't scratch that itch ourselves, we like reading about someone else who could and did.

This passage (which one suspects that many Christians have never read or pondered) declares that we must find quite different ways of dealing with the problem. Revenge is ruled out. Instead, we are to find creative, surprising new ways of dealing with people who hurt us. This is a huge challenge. Getting our moral wills around this one is every bit as difficult as getting our minds around some of the trickier bits of Paul's writing in the earlier chapters. But here it is in black and white.

We should note that this does *not* mean 'going soft on evil'. Saying you shouldn't take revenge isn't a way of saying evil isn't real, or that it didn't hurt after all, or that it doesn't matter. Evil *is* real; it often *does* hurt, sometimes very badly indeed and with lasting effects, and it *does* matter. This is, perhaps, one of the fundamental differences between Christianity and, say, Buddhism. Because we believe in a creator God who made a good and lovely world, we believe that everything which defaces and distorts, damages or spoils part of that creation is not just another variety of goodness but is actually its opposite, evil. The question is, what are we going to do about it?

79

For Paul, that question begins with the question, what has God done about it? Quite a bit of the letter, earlier on, has been devoted to answering this question, and it boils down to what he says in 5.6–11: while we were still sinners, the **Messiah** died for us. There are many other things to be said about God's moral governance of the world, but at the centre of the Christian story stands this claim, that when human evil reached its height God came and took its full weight upon himself, thereby exhausting it and opening the way for the creation of a new world altogether. Revenge keeps evil in circulation. Whether in a family or a town, or in an entire community like the Middle East or Northern Ireland, the culture of revenge, unless broken, is never-ending. Both sides will always be able to 'justify' further atrocities by reference to those they themselves have suffered.

This brings us to the question of whether it is possible to forgive someone who isn't sorry. I had a letter from a small boy the other day asking me exactly that question; it's something that even very young children can understand, and they are often just as good as adults in thinking about such problems. This passage seems to indicate that, though when someone isn't sorry there is no chance of full reconciliation, it is not only possible but actually commanded that we should rid ourselves of any desire for revenge. Instead, we should actually go out of our way to do positive, uncalled-for acts of kindness to those who have wronged us. That, in turn, may lead them at least to remorse (that is probably what the reference to 'burning coals' in verse 20, quoting Proverbs 25.21, is all about), or even to **repentance** and thereby to reconciliation.

Whatever the effect, though, part of the point is that when we refuse to take revenge, and deliberately rid ourselves even of the desire for it, we are taking responsibility at least for our own mental and emotional health. We are refusing to allow our own future lives to be determined by the evil that someone else has done. It's bad enough that they've done whatever it was; why should they then have the right to keep us in a bitter and twisted state? That's what Paul means by 'letting evil conquer you'.

This passage, of course, needs to be balanced by the next one, at the start of chapter 13. There, as we shall see, Paul takes a strong line on the importance of the governing authorities doing their job. But the point is that rulers and legitimate authorities do not act as private individuals. If a judge, or a member of a jury, is known to have a personal involvement or interest in the case, that should automatically disqualify them from sitting. Rulers frequently *must* do what private individuals *may not* do; and if rulers don't do it, then private individuals may get fed up waiting to see justice done and take the law into their own hands, making chaos come again and reducing society to the rule of the most powerful.

Whether or not the rulers deal with the matter, however, part of the point is that we should trust God to deal with it in his own time and way. That's what Paul means by 'allow God's anger room to work' in verse 19. God has his own ways of bringing people to their senses and of letting them feel the results of their own folly or wickedness. It isn't up to us (except insofar as we may be called to act as magistrates or other public officials, as in 13.1–7) to hurry that process along or anticipate it.

The whole passage, in fact, is about how Christians behave within the wider public world. The previous verses dealt with what we might call the inner life of the church;

now Paul turns to its outward appearance. Even with those who explicitly persecute the church, the right response is not cursing, but blessing. This represents a major step beyond the accepted norms within the Judaism of the time. Did Paul, we wonder, have in mind Jesus' prayer for the people crucifying him, recorded in Luke 23.34? The command to celebrate and mourn (verse 15) with those who are happy or sad doesn't just refer to other church members; Christians are to be known as good neighbours, prepared to join in the fun when someone on the street has good news, and to be there to support and weep alongside those who face tragedy. It is within that kind of setting, where Christians are known, liked and respected, that people will be prepared to listen to them talking about the Lord they serve, the one who seemed to let evil conquer him when he died on the cross but who, in fact, overcame it with the power of his own love and life.

ROMANS 13.1–7

The Divine Purpose, and Limited Role, of Ruling Authorities

[1]Every person must be subject to the ruling authorities. There is no authority, you see, except from God, and those that exist have been put in place by God. [2]As a result, anyone who rebels against authority is resisting what God has set up, and those who resist will bring judgment on themselves. [3]For rulers hold no terrors for people who do good, but only for people who do evil.

If you want to have no fear of the ruling power, do what is good, and it will praise you. [4]It is God's servant, you see: for you and your good. But if you do evil, be afraid; the

82

sword it carries is no empty gesture. It is God's servant, in fact, to bring his anger on evildoers. [5]That is why it is necessary to submit, not only to avoid punishment but because of conscience.

[6]That, too, is why you pay taxes. The officials in question are God's ministers, attending to this very thing. [7]So pay each of them what is owed: tribute to those who collect it, revenue to those who collect it. Respect those who should be respected. Honour the people one ought to honour.

When you hear the word 'policeman', what is your instant reaction?

For many people growing up in Britain when I was young, the policeman was a friendly and familiar figure. (There weren't many police*women* around then.) He could be stern when he needed to be, but you knew he was on your side. He wanted to help, to protect people from danger and evil. You could walk up to him and ask the time, or the way, and get a friendly smile as well as the right advice. He was there to make sure all was well, to enable ordinary people to go about their business.

What about the word 'taxman'? (Again, there weren't many tax*women* when I was growing up.) That's a bit harder. The first time I was conscious of the word it was said as a kind of warning: so and so works for the tax authorities, so be careful what you say to him or we'll end up paying more money than we should.

What about words like 'government', or 'the council'? In many countries, including many in the democratic Western world where we elect our governments and our local councils, many citizens have become cynical about their elected representatives, particularly as a whole (there may be some good people among them, but taken together we tend to get frustrated, or worse, at what they do or don't do). And that attitude now increasingly applies to police as well, even in Britain. In several countries, of course, the police have always been feared or even hated, even by people with nothing to hide.

That makes it all the more remarkable, to many readers today, that Paul wrote this little paragraph about the ruling authorities. Many today take it for granted that rulers are not to be trusted. Many Christians take it for granted that governments are corrupt and dehumanizing, and that it's part of our brief as followers of the Lord Jesus, the world's true sovereign, that we should offer serious criticism and opposition, even, if necessary, at a cost to our own prospects. When we add to this the fact that Paul was writing during the first century of the Roman Empire, currently ruled by the notorious Nero (Nero's early years were not as bad as his later ones, but the system he ran was full of injustice and imperial arrogance, and had been for a long time), some people find it so incredible to think of Paul writing this that they wonder if maybe the paragraph has been stuck into the letter by someone else. Other people think that this may have been a topic Paul hadn't given much thought to at this stage, but that by the time he wrote later letters from prison he had changed his mind about whether Roman authority was such a good thing.

These explanations are not convincing. Indeed, they miss the point of what's going on. Of course, this paragraph has been used – and abused – by many people in power as a way of telling their subjects to keep silent and offer no resistance even in the face of flagrant abuse. That was the line taken by many white people, particularly rulers, during the apartheid regime in South Africa. Like many passages in the Bible, a few verses taken out of context can become dangerous and misleading.

When we put these verses back into their context, right here in the letter, we start to see what Paul is getting at. He has just said, strongly and repeatedly, that private vengeance is absolutely forbidden for Christians. But this doesn't mean, on the one hand, that God doesn't care about evil, or, on the other, that God wants society to collapse into a chaos where the bullies and the power-brokers do what they like and get away with it. In fact, even in countries where people hate the authorities and fear the police, when someone commits a murder or even a serious robbery, everybody affected by it wants good authorities and good police who will find the culprit and administer justice. That is a basic, and correct, human instinct. We don't want to live by the law of the jungle. We want to live as human beings in an ordered, properly functioning society.

That is almost all that Paul is saying, making the point as he does so that the Christians, who were regarded as the scum of the earth in Rome at the time, must not get an additional reputation as trouble-makers. No good will come to the cause of the **gospel** by followers of Jesus being regarded as crazy dissidents who won't co-operate with the most basic social mechanisms. Paul is anxious, precisely because he believes that Jesus is the true Lord of the world, that his followers should not pick unnecessary quarrels with the lesser lords. They are indeed a revolutionary community, but if they go for the normal type of violent revolution they will just be playing the empire back at its own game. They will almost certainly lose, and, much worse, the gospel itself will lose with them.

But, while making this point, Paul is making one or two others of great interest. To begin with, he declares that the civic rulers and authorities have been put in place by God himself. This would be news to Nero and the other emperors, who believed (or claimed to believe) in their own divinity, certainly that they held power in their own right rather than as a gift from the One Creator God, the God of Israel. They would have laughed at such a suggestion. The Christians are called to believe, though, that the civic authorities, great and small, are there because the one true God wants his world to be ordered, not chaotic. This does not validate particular actions of particular governments. It is merely to say that *some* government is always necessary, in a world where evil flourishes when unchecked.

Of course Paul knew that quite often one might do the right thing and find the rulers doing the wrong thing. You only have to read the stories of his escapades in Acts to see that. But notice, in those stories (his visit to Philippi in Acts 16, for instance, or his trial before the Jewish authorities in Acts 23), that precisely when the authorities are getting it all wrong and acting illegally or unjustly, Paul has no hesitation in telling them their proper business and insisting that they should follow it. Hardly the way to become popular, but completely consistent with what he says here.

His comments about taxes may well have a specific point in relation to the Roman situation at the time. Roman subjects living in the capital paid two types of tax, some direct and some indirect. The latter was so unpopular that it led to riots about this time, and at one point Nero actually promised the people of Rome that he would cancel all indirect taxation. (Cynics today will not be surprised to hear that he didn't keep the promise.) Clearly those who believed that Jesus was the one true Lord of the world might well use that belief to rationalize withholding taxes which many of their pagan contemporaries, too, thought were unjust. Paul stands out against that. Christians were likely to get into quite enough trouble for far more serious things, as he knew well from his own experience; but they should be good citizens as far as they can.

In saying this Paul was standing within a particular Jewish tradition, and developing it in the light of the gospel. The Old Testament had denounced pagan nations and their rulers – but some of the very prophets whose denunciations were fiercest also told Israel that God was working *through* the pagan nations and their rulers for Israel's long-term good (Assyria, in Isaiah 10; Cyrus, in Isaiah 45; Babylon itself, in Jeremiah 29). The long centuries before the coming of Jesus saw many Jewish attempts to hold together the firm belief that their God, the creator, was in fact sovereign over the nations with the equally firm belief that the pagan nations, and often enough their rulers, were wicked, idolatrous, immoral and dangerous for Israel. It was precisely this tension which came to its head when, in John's story, Jesus stood before the Roman governor and declared that, even though he was about to execute him, the power by which he did it had come from God in the first place (John 19.11).

There are complexities here we cannot delve into further. As we note that fact, we should also note that it is high time to awaken the older traditions of Christian political thought which have been dormant in the Western church for the last two hundred years or so. It isn't a matter of the easy-going 'left/right' spectrum of politics we so often assume in the modern world, with the gospel on one side or the other. Life is more complicated, and interesting, than that. As we face the serious decline of democracy (as witnessed, for instance, by the shockingly low turnout of voters) in many countries that pride themselves on it, Christians today need urgently to consider what it means *both* that God wants his world to be governed under the rule of appropriate law *and* that Jesus is already installed as the supreme Lord of **heaven** and earth.

ROMANS 13.8–14

Love, the Law and the Coming Day

⁸Don't owe anything to anyone, except the debt of mutual love. If you love your neighbour, you see, you have fulfilled the law. ⁹Commandments like 'don't commit adultery, don't kill, don't steal, don't covet' – and any other commandment – are summed up in this: 'Love your neighbour as yourself.' ¹⁰Love does no wrong to its neighbour; so love is the fulfilment of the law.

¹¹This is all the more important because you know what time it is. The hour has come for you to wake up from sleep. Our salvation, you see, is nearer now than it was when first we came to faith. ¹²The night is nearly over, the day is almost here. So let's put off the works of darkness, and put on the armour of light. ¹³Let's behave appropriately, as in the daytime: not in wild parties and drunkenness, not in orgies and shameless immorality, not in bad temper and jealousy. ¹⁴Instead, put on the Lord Jesus, the Messiah, and don't make any allowance for the flesh and its lusts.

When I was at boarding school, I often used to wake up early on summer mornings as the daylight came streaming in from four or five o'clock onwards. I often used to think how silly it was not to get up then. Frequently the day would be bright and sunny until about the middle of the morning, when clouds would roll in and spoil it. Often it would rain later on, despite the bright early sunshine. As a keen sportsman, I used to get cross at having games spoiled by rain when I knew that, if we'd been out playing before breakfast, we might have had several hours in the sunshine. We could always have done our schoolwork once the rain set in. Why wouldn't my friends wake up so that we could go out and start the match?

This sense, that it's important to be waking up and getting ahead of the day, is what Paul is picking up in this passage, rather as he does in 1 Thessalonians 5. He is expanding what he said quite densely in 12.1–2. The old world, the '**present age**', is rumbling on. Most people are ordering their lives in accordance with its style and habits. But the new world has already broken in. God's new age has begun, and will shortly come to fulfilment. Those who follow Jesus, whose life, death and **resurrection** inaugurated that new age, are commanded to live already according to the rules of the new world. The day has begun, even though most people are still asleep.

Paul's instructions for what this daytime behaviour will mean are quite specific and very bracing. Night-time is when people get drunk, go to wild parties and do all kinds of things they would be ashamed of in broad daylight. Very well; that kind of behaviour must go, however fashionable it may be. Night-time is when people feel free to indulge in shameless sexual immorality. That must be ruled out as well.

By this point in verse 13 Paul is heading for a list of types of bad behaviour rather than a list of nocturnal activities.

He contents himself with one more double prohibition which has nothing to do with the ordinary contrast of night and day: bad temper and jealousy, alas, can be just as common during the day as the night, perhaps more so. The analogy, but not the point, has broken down. For the Christian, anger and bitterness are just as much forbidden as drunkenness and off-limits sexual activity, though you wouldn't think so from many churches.

But he doesn't just tell people what to avoid. He shows them *how* to avoid it. 'Put on the Lord Jesus, the **Messiah**', he says. What does that mean? How can we do it?

'Putting on' comes from the night/day contrast once more. Here we are, getting up while the rest of the world still thinks it's night-time; we must put our clothes on. The Christian's 'clothing' – which two verses earlier he has referred to as 'armour', the 'armour of light', the clothing we need when the light has begun to shine – consists of Jesus himself, Jesus the Lord, Jesus the king. I know some Christians who in their private devotions each day make a conscious effort in prayer to 'clothe themselves' with the very character of Jesus. Some people do this by reading, slowly, a story from the **gospels**, and praying that the character of the Jesus they meet there will surround them, protect them, and be the thing that other people see when they meet them. For other people it's a regular discipline of remembering their **baptism**, the time when they were plunged into the water as a sign of dying with the Messiah, and brought up out of it as a sign of rising again with him, so that (as in Romans 6) they are no longer living in the old world, but in the new. This, indeed, is the heart of what is sometimes called Paul's 'ethic': the new world is here, those who belong to Jesus belong to it, therefore they must live by its standards rather than by the present ones of society.

But, someone will say, surely Paul thought the world was coming to an end very soon? Doesn't he say in verse 11 that salvation is about to burst upon the world? And if he was wrong about that, might he not have been wrong about the new day dawning at all?

It is important to stress that Paul did *not* believe, in that sense, that the world was about to come to an end. When he says in 2 Thessalonians 2 that the Christians in Thessalonica mustn't be worried if they get a letter saying that the Day of the Lord had arrived, it is clear that this Day cannot have involved the end of the world. If it had – to put it no more strongly – the Thessalonians would have noticed. Clearly Paul seems to have thought of great crises that were coming, as we might put it, *within* history, not simply to end it. What he has said about the coming new world in Romans 8.18–27 indicates clearly enough that the new world will be the liberation of the present world, not its abolition. Finally, it's noticeable that, right through the next century and beyond, Christian teachers went on telling people that God's new world was dawning. It didn't matter to them that it hadn't happened within Paul's lifetime or shortly afterwards.

In fact, the point Paul and the other early Christians were making is not that the final day of salvation is bound to happen within a *short* time. The event to happen within a generation, in Mark 13 and elsewhere, was the destruction of Jerusalem, which did indeed come to pass in AD 70. The point was that the day might come at *any* time. This was because the event which prepared the way for it, the resurrection of Jesus, had already happened. God's new world had been launched. The sun was already rising, and it was time to get up. It didn't matter precisely how many hours were left before the whole world was flooded with light.

In this in-between time, where Christians are commanded to live in the present world as citizens of the future one, the time of fulfilment of God's promises means also the time of fulfilment of God's **law** (verses 8–10). This 'fulfilment' has nothing whatever to do with people keeping the law in order to earn either God's favour or their membership within God's people or any special status. It simply has to do with them responding to God's mercy and love (12.1) in the most appropriate way possible, by loving the way of **life** which reflects God's own character – loving it, indeed, in a way which those who have not known God's love and saving grace cannot understand or appreciate (8.6–8).

Here Paul uses this idea of fulfilling the law, and of doing so in particular through love, as part of his appeal to the Christians in Rome to live attractive lives in the local community, surrounded as they are by the watching stares of puzzled pagans. Don't get in debt to anyone, he says – a warning our present Western society has done its best to ignore over the last generation – except to regard yourself in debt to everyone, to love them. If you love them you won't commit murder. If you love them you won't steal from them. If you love them you will be delighted that this man has plenty to live on, that this woman has that fine dress, that this couple live in that attractive house; you won't covet what they have, because you will be glad for them. (Covetousness, we recall, was the point at which the 'I' in Romans 7 recognized its own inability to keep the law; see 7.7–8.)

And, we note, if you love your neighbour you won't commit adultery. English speakers have got into such trouble over the word 'love'. It's a perfectly good word, but it has been made to do too many jobs, covering *both* the selfless and self-giving love Paul is speaking of here, which denies its own desires in order to do the best thing for its neighbour, *and* the thoroughly selfish pursuit of one's own desire for another person's body irrespective of consequences. We might call the second type 'lust', but nobody who falls helplessly in love (as we like to put it) with someone else's spouse likes to call it 'lust': this person is so attractive, so exciting, so interesting . . . it must be 'love', and doesn't the Bible say that as long as you love, that's what matters?

We can see how easily people argue like that with themselves, and sometimes even with their spiritual directors and counsellors, but Paul would have made short work of it. The point of love, genuine Christian love, what the New Testament writers call *agapē* (though some Greek writers used this word, too, in a wider sense like the English 'love'), was that it meant copying the self-giving love of Jesus himself. This love is included in the command to 'put on' Jesus, as in verse 14. And in that self-giving love there is no room for immorality, particularly for cheating in marriage, your own or someone else's – however much it tries to disguise itself as 'love'. The watching pagan world of the first century would have known what to make of that. In fact, for another century at least it was one of the proudest boasts the early church could make to the watching world that Christians were not sexually immoral. Would that we could make that boast today.

ROMANS 14.1–6

The Weak and the Strong

¹Welcome someone who is weak in faith, but not in order to have disputes on difficult points. ²One person believes it is all right to eat anything, while the weak person eats only vegetables. ³The one who eats should not despise the one who does not, and the one who does not should not condemn the one who does – because God has welcomed them.

⁴Who do you think you are to judge someone else's servants? They stand or fall before their own master. And stand they will, because the master can make them stand.

⁵One person reckons one day more important than another. Someone else regards all days as equally important. Each person must make up their own mind. ⁶The one who celebrates the day does so in honour of the Lord, just as the one who eats does so in honour of the Lord, since they give thanks to God. The one who does not eat, too, is abstaining in honour of the Lord, and likewise gives thanks to God.

We have a friend whose son is a vegetarian. She was describing to us today how she has learned to cook special meals for him – and what sort of compromises with the code he has been prepared to make. In today's Western world, vegetarianism has become a serious option for millions. Restaurants now routinely offer vegetarian options. This was almost unknown when I was young.

The ancient world knew about vegetarianism, too, but often people took that option for quite different reasons from those we think of today. Hardly anyone in Paul's world thought it cruel to slaughter animals for food. Most people at the time lived very close to the means of food production, whether animals or crops, and thought no more of killing a cow or a pig than of picking an olive off a tree. No: the reason why some people in Paul's world, certainly the ones he's talking about in this chapter, became vegetarian was because they couldn't guarantee getting the right *sort* of meat. Would it be pure? Granted they were allowed to eat meat, were they allowed to eat *this* meat? Had it been slaughtered in the proper manner? Had it been cooked in the right way?

This is similar to the problem Paul faced in 1 Corinthians 8, but perhaps with a further twist as well. There, the question had to do with meat that had been offered to an idol, that is, slaughtered as a **sacrifice** in a pagan temple and then either served up in the adjoining restaurant or offered for sale in the market. No devout Jew would dream of eating such meat. Many of the early Christians, too, having been regular attenders at pagan temples before their conversion, and knowing full well the kind of lifestyle that went with it all, avoided anything that reminded them of it. That was the context in which Paul insisted equally (a) that, since God was the creator, all meat was good in itself and therefore could in principle be eaten, and (b) that if someone else's conscience was being hurt, even those who had a robust conscience about eating the food should abstain from doing so.

In the present chapter that discussion has broadened out a bit, probably to include those Jews who would become vegetarians in practice because, in their part of the city, they could not guarantee being able to get meat that had been properly slaughtered according to the 'kosher' laws laid down in the Bible and interpreted in Jewish tradition. Unless there was a proper Jewish butcher available, it might well have seemed the wiser course to abstain not only from pork, as Jews would anyway (though pork was the cheapest and most readily available meat in that world), but from all meat of whatever kind.

What is fascinating about this whole chapter is that, though it seems clear that the issues Paul is talking about are things that would have divided Jewish Christians from **Gentile** Christians, he does *not* say, 'Many Jewish Christians don't eat meat, and many Gentile Christians do.' For a start, there were plenty of Jewish Christians – himself included – who were what he calls 'strong', that is, who had worked it out and settled it in their mind that all foods were now 'clean'. There were probably some Gentile Christians, too, like the ones in Galatia, who in their eagerness to avoid the ugly memories of their pagan background had embraced not only the Christian ethic but the strict Jewish rules as well. But there is a deeper reason, I think, why Paul simply says, 'Some of us do it this way, some of us do it that way.'

His reason, I think, is that he is precisely trying to break down the walls which the early Christians so easily put up between people of different ethnic origin. If he'd said 'Jewish Christians do this, Gentile Christians do that,' he would simply have been reinforcing the barriers he was trying to get them to forget. It's only in chapter 15 that the underlying agenda becomes clear, and then at the point where (at 15.8) he is appealing to them to worship together. For the moment he is trying to educate them to look at one another, not as 'Oh, he's Jewish', or, 'Oh, she's Gentile', but as *fellow servants of the same master, fellow* **disciples** *of the same Lord*. In fact, the word for 'master' and 'Lord' in these verses is the same, so that even when Paul is using the metaphor of servants and their master in verse 4 he is already hinting at the point he makes in verse 6, and will continue to make again and again throughout the passage.

What we are dealing with in this passage is in fact the direct consequence of Paul's doctrine of **justification by faith,** which he has of course expounded at length earlier in the letter. Jews and Gentiles who believe in Jesus are welcomed equally because of Jesus' own achievement in his death and **resurrection**. They are marked out solely by their belief that he is Lord, and that God raised him from the dead (10.9–13, a passage which Paul seems to be echoing at various points in this chapter). They must therefore learn to live together without looking down their noses at one another or implying for a moment that God is more pleased with one style of behaviour than with another. Paul does not seem to be suggesting here that there was in Rome a problem of the same magnitude as the one he had faced in Antioch (Galatians 2.11–21). But that might be only because the different Christian groups in Rome were scattered and not even attempting to come together for meals or worship, whereas at least in Antioch they had been doing so.

Nor was it only food that was causing the potential problem. It was the keeping of holy days (verses 5 and 6). Pagan societies kept special feast days and holidays, of course, but Paul is probably referring to Jewish practices. Some Christians would keep the major Jewish festivals; others would not. For Paul it had become a point of indifference. What mattered was that whichever decision you made, you did what you did in honour of the Lord. (Someone today who lounged in bed on a Sunday morning, claiming that Paul said it didn't matter, would I suspect get a sharp retort from the **apostle**.)

So what is the situation in Rome, and what does Paul expect them to do? By starting off with an instruction to welcome the 'weak in faith', he seems to be assuming that most of the Christians are 'strong', probably Gentile Christians, quite likely people who had been converted through his own work further east and had now travelled to Rome. Some people in that category are named in chapter 16. These people, it seems, would have agreed with Paul that a Christian could in principle eat anything.

By 'weak in faith' he doesn't mean that the religious devotion of this group is thin and watery. Nor does he mean to imply that they have a shaky grasp on the basic points of Christian faith, or a wavering belief in them. His point, rather, is that they have not worked out, or not as fully as he and some others have done, the consequences of believing in God as creator and Jesus as the crucified and risen Lord. For Paul, believing this meant that all foods were now 'clean' (as Mark 7.19 points out that Jesus had implied) and that, though keeping holy days might help devotion, a Christian was free to observe special days or not, provided this was done with a desire to honour the Lord.

Paul continues to develop this argument in the passages which follow. But for now it may be worth taking a minute to ponder possible parallels in our own day. At what points in today's church are we in danger of judging one another because of things that Paul would declare to be indifferent? Where are we prone to build walls of division on cultural or ethnic lines where Paul would gently but firmly insist that we are all serving the same master?

ROMANS 14.7–12

The Final Judgment Is the Only One that Counts

[7]None of us lives to ourselves; none of us dies to ourselves. [8]If we live, we live to the Lord, and if we die, we die to the Lord. So, then, whether we live or whether we die, we belong to the Lord. [9]That is why the Messiah died and came back to life, so that he might be Lord both of the dead and of the living.

[10]You, then: why do you condemn your fellow Christian? Or you: why do you despise a fellow Christian? We must all appear before the judgment seat of God, [11]as the Bible says:

> As I live, says the Lord, to me every knee shall bow,
> and every tongue shall give praise to God.

[12]So then, we must each give an account of ourselves to God.

As I pondered this passage, a verse from an old 1960s song came into my mind:

> And they argue through the night:
> Black is black, and white is white;
> Then walk away both knowing they are right.
> And nobody's buying flowers
> From the flower lady.

The singer was the late Phil Ochs, complaining there not simply (as he usually did) about the perceived follies of his day, but also about the difficulty, which has become more apparent since he wrote, of bringing two opposing positions within talking distance of one another. I am reminded of a comment by another old cynic, the philosopher Bertrand Russell. In his autobiography he describes a moment where he and his wife had to make a difficult decision. I can't remember which of them got their way, but he says, looking back after many years, 'I still think I was right, and she still thinks she was right.'

This is what's going on in verse 10. Paul is addressing a situation which will be depressingly familiar to many who work within the church as well as many who work outside it. In this verse he seems to turn from one party to the other. Here is a Christian with a strict conscience, whose background, upbringing and temperament all incline him towards a very serious view of his moral responsibilities. As far as he can see (and that phrase is important), the Christian is surrounded by a very wicked, corrupt pagan world. The best thing to do is to shun it completely; and if that means not touching meat, so be it. He then notices that this woman over here, who apparently claims to be a Christian as well, is buying, from the market, meat which has obviously come from a pagan temple. How appalling! She's letting the side down! She and her family are deeply compromised! The only response is condemnation.

The Christian woman, meanwhile, has been taught the deep and rich truth that the one true God is the creator and redeemer of all things. The whole world belongs to him, including every piece of meat you might ever buy or cook. She knows perfectly well that she is called to holiness, to a lifestyle very different from that of the pagan world around. But she knows equally well (perhaps she has been reading the closing paragraphs of Colossians 2) that outward regulations about what you can and can't touch, taste and handle don't actually go to the heart of genuine holiness. For that you need the complete renewal spoken of at the start of Colossians 3. She gets tired of being sniped at and criticized by people who don't seem to have learned what is, for her, one of the most basic and liberating of the gospel's lessons. They seem small minded, timid, unable to see beyond their own front doors. When she thinks of people like that, she despises them.

Both are natural reactions. Each grows out of a firm grasp of one part of Christian truth. But towering above the truths that these two characters have embraced there stands a further truth which needs to be grasped even more firmly, and lived out even more energetically: that there is one Lord, and it is before him and him alone that every Christian lives and dies, stands or falls. This is the great emphasis of this particular paragraph.

The church seems to need to learn this lesson over and over again, often in respect of new and different issues. Precisely for this reason, giving examples is difficult, since part of the question is always whether *this* issue actually is a case in point, or whether it is something about which there can be no two opinions. Let's pick two extreme cases to make the point.

Supposing a Christian were to say, 'I know the Old Testament tells us not to steal; but Paul says in 1 Corinthians 3.21 that "All things are yours!", and I think that means we should be free to help ourselves to anything we want. I know some people still have a tender conscience about such things, and I respect that; but I hope they will respect me too. I won't despise them for their small-minded legalism if they won't condemn me for my liberty in the gospel.' I think most of us would be able to answer such a person, and at the heart of our answer would be the comment that stealing or not stealing is *not* one of the things about which Christians can legitimately differ. It is forbidden. The Old Testament prohibition is powerfully reinforced in the New.

On the other hand, supposing a Christian were to read the book of Leviticus, and to discover there a clear command forbidding the wearing of clothes made from two different kinds of material (Leviticus 19.19). Someone with a tender conscience might feel morally obliged to go through their whole wardrobe, sorting out clothes made from one material only and throwing all the others away. We might even suppose (I said these were going to be extreme examples) that the person then began a protest movement, organizing pickets outside shops that sold the wrong kind of clothes and encouraging Christian friends to join in, as a witness to biblical morality. We can imagine the attitudes not only of non-Christians looking on, but of Christians of virtually every kind. Why are you making a fuss about that? Surely God isn't concerned about the fact that the shirt I'm wearing is made from cotton and polyester? Did Jesus or Paul or any of the early Christians say anything about such a trivial matter? Get a life!

In the first case, there would be almost universal agreement that stealing is *not* a matter about which we can say, 'Some of us believe this, others believe that, so we mustn't condemn or despise one another.' In the second, we would almost all want to say that mixing fabrics in clothes is a matter of complete indifference. The question is, how can you tell? How do we know which issues come into which category?

This is a huge question, and the only way to answer it is to go back through not only Romans but also the gospels and the rest of the New Testament and weigh carefully, case by case, what is said and, equally importantly, the reasons why it is said. We cannot and must not use the 'Let's agree to differ' line as a way of avoiding the challenge of, for instance, Romans 6.1–14, 8.12–17 or 12.1–2. And the present passage sends us back to a principle which, though Paul doesn't often emphasize it, remains at the heart of all his thinking: Jesus, the **Messiah**, has been appointed by God to be the judge of the living and the dead, and one day this judgment will search out and test the entire life of every man, woman and child.

This is what Isaiah had said, in a passage which was obviously a favourite of Paul's (45.23, quoted again in Philippians 2.10). Nothing in the New Testament – not the principle of free grace, not **justification** by **faith**, not the infinite mercy of God – undermines it. Indeed, it is re-emphasized again and again (to look no further than Paul, we might compare Romans 2.1–16, 2 Corinthians 5.10 and, on a slightly different point, 1 Corinthians 3.10–17). Final judgment matters because God is committed to putting the whole world to rights; God will judge through Jesus the Messiah, calling each of us to account. Judgment has already begun with God's condemnation of sin on the cross and his raising of Jesus to new **life**. We live between that event and the final judgment, *and everything we do happens in that light.* We do not live to ourselves; we do not die to ourselves. It isn't up to us what we do and don't do. It is up to the Lord, the master whom we serve and who will one day require an account.

The mutual respect for which Paul is calling is therefore one vital aspect of the doctrine of justification by faith itself. Justification, we will recall from the earlier chapters of the letter, is about God *anticipating in the present* the verdict which will be announced in the future (3.21–26; 10.9–13). All those who believe in Jesus the Messiah, the risen Lord, are declared already in the present to be forgiven sinners, to be in the right, to belong to the one renewed people of God. Paul is now appealing for Christians from all backgrounds to make this a reality in their present common life. God has declared both this person and that person to be members of his people. They stand before their maker and their Lord, and must take responsibility for themselves (see too Galatians 6.5). Christians must learn to respect one another, and to find ways of living out in practice what it means to live to the Lord and to die to the Lord.

ROMANS 14.13–23

The Way of Love and Peace

[13]Do not, then, pass judgment on one another. If you want to exercise your judgment, do so on this question: how to avoid placing obstacles or stumbling blocks in front of a fellow family member.

[14]I know, and am persuaded in the Lord Jesus, that nothing is unclean in itself; but things do become unclean for the person who regards them as such. [15]For if your brother or sister is being harmed by what you eat, you are no longer behaving in accordance with love. Don't let your food destroy someone for whom the Messiah died!

[16]So don't let something that is good for you make other people blaspheme. [17]God's kingdom, you see, isn't about food and drink, but about justice, peace, and joy in the holy spirit. [18]Anyone who serves the Messiah like this pleases God and deserves respect from other people. [19]So, then, let's find and follow the way of peace, and discover

how to build each other up. ²⁰Don't pull down God's work on account of food. Everything is pure, but it becomes evil for anyone who causes offence when they eat. ²¹It is good not to eat meat, or drink wine, or anything else which makes your fellow Christian stumble.

²²Hold firmly to the faith which you have as a matter between yourself and God. When you've thought something through, and can go ahead without passing judgment on yourself, God's blessing on you! ²³But anyone who doubts is condemned even in the act of eating, because it doesn't spring from faith. Whatever is not of faith is sin.

The snow was heavy that night – so heavy that by the time they opened the curtains they could only just see the top of the garden gate. There must have been at least three feet of the stuff.

At the breakfast table, the son reminded his father that he'd promised to give him some work to do around the place to earn some extra pocket money.

'All right,' said his father. 'We're going to have to get out of the front gate. I think you could start by digging out the path.'

The son, eager for his pay, put on his boots and coat, grabbed the shovel, and began work. He was fit and strong and soon got into the swing of it. Shovelfuls of snow flew this way and that. He kept his head down, concentrating on making a good, complete job of it. Eventually he stood up, drew breath and looked with satisfaction down the length of the path. You could now walk all the way from the house to the gate. You wouldn't even slip.

His father came out.

'Well done,' he said. 'Come and have a cup of coffee and get your pay.'

But as they were going inside they heard a voice.

'Then will you come and clear away all the extra snow you've put on *my* path?'

It was the next-door neighbour, standing at his door, looking not only at his snowy front garden but at all the snow that had been shovelled so energetically, and that had flown so gracefully off one path and onto another.

Father and son looked at each other. The neighbour wasn't cross, indeed he was amused, but clearly something had to be done.

'I think that looks like a two-man job,' said the father.

Paul's supreme concern in this passage is the danger of so clearing your own path that you end up making it impossible for your neighbours to walk down theirs. It is all too easy, in sorting out our own lives and finding our own way forward as Christians, to make things harder, not easier, for those around us. Since one of the basic Jewish and Christian images for what we call 'behaviour' is that of 'walking', a natural way of describing these difficulties is the one Paul highlights in verse 13: the danger of putting 'obstacles' or 'stumbling blocks' – things that will trip people up – in each other's way.

So, he says with deliberate humour, don't pass judgment on each other – but *do* use your judgment in not tripping each other up! Just as it is vital for every Christian to make up his or her mind about things which are, as we saw in the previous passage, 'indifferent' – things about which Christians can legitimately differ – so it is vital that, when we have done so, our main concern is then not for ourselves but for those around us. Other people may well be at a different point in the Christian life, and may still be struggling with their conscience over things which we believe to be perfectly good in themselves. There is of course a case for Christian education so that, bit by bit, people can work through scruples and problems of conscience. Paul isn't talking about that. It won't do to say, as we are sometimes tempted to, 'Well, they should grow up and stop fussing about such trivia.' That can easily result in a clear path for us and a pile of extra snow for them. And that's not the way to make friends with the neighbours, still less to live as brothers and sisters in the Christian family.

The way forward is to recognize that things can and do become unclean, or even evil, not because of what they are in themselves but because of how people regard them. This is rather like saying that beauty is in the eye of the beholder, and it's obviously not a principle which can be applied to all ethical questions and situations. Paul is talking specifically about what people eat and drink, in a context where that was very contentious. We have to use wise judgment ourselves, as we saw in the previous passage, as to which of today's issues come into the picture at this point. What he says in verse 14 is that food can and does *become* unclean – at the point at which someone considers it so; and, in verse 20, that it can and does become *evil* (a stage beyond 'unclean') if when you eat it you cause someone else to trip up.

This whole passage is, in fact, looking one way in the argument. It is an appeal to people who are happy to eat and drink anything at all. It is asking them to recognize that there are occasions when they need to hold back from this freedom for the sake of those whose Christian **faith** would be irreparably damaged by such behaviour.

As we saw at the start of the chapter, Paul is in all probability appealing to **Gentile** Christians to exercise restraint in the way they behave, so as not to alienate or antagonize Jewish Christians. This is in line with things he has said throughout the letter. Whereas in Galatians he had to warn Gentile Christians against taking the Jewish **law** on to themselves to try to consolidate their membership in the **Messiah**'s family, here the boot is on the other foot.

If we are correct in assuming that he is writing Romans not long after the Jews had returned to Rome in AD 54, we can see why this appeal would be urgently necessary. Jewish Christians, seeing Gentile Christians in Rome doing things which from their point of view were associated with paganism, might look on in horror. They might conclude that they had made an awful mistake, call down curses on this new movement (verse 16), and give up the faith altogether.

If that were to happen, Paul declares, it would be an offence against nothing less than the death of the Messiah (verse 15), undoing the work he accomplished on the cross. It would be a reversal of priorities (verse 17), focusing attention on food and drink instead of on the major, towering realities of God's **kingdom**: justice, peace and joy. It would be to pull down the house which God is so carefully building up (verse 20).

The last two verses of the chapter offer a stern test for how faith must work out in practice. The point of verse 23 is not so much a warning to people to be sure they are acting from pure and complete motives of faith, though it serves as that as well. It is, more specifically, a warning to the people indicted in verse 22, the people who have thought through the relevant issues and are happy to consume all kinds of food and drink: don't put *other* people in the position of verse 23. Don't insist that all other Christians conform at once to the freedom which you celebrate. Don't force them to walk through your snow. It will take a good deal of thought and prayer to apply these lessons to today's and tomorrow's issues in the church, but the more we work our way into Paul's mind in Romans 14 the better we shall be equipped to do so.

ROMANS 15.1–6

Unity: Modelled by the Messiah, Encouraged by Scripture

[1]We, the 'strong' ones, should bear with the frailty of the 'weak', and not please ourselves. [2]Each one of us should please our neighbour for his or her good, to build them up.

[3]The Messiah, you see, did not please himself. Instead, as the Bible says, 'the reproaches of those who reproached you are fallen on me'. [4]Whatever was written ahead of time, you see, was written for us to learn from, so that through patience, and through the encouragement of the Bible, we might have hope. [5]May the God of patience and encouragement grant you to come to a common mind among yourselves, in accordance with the Messiah, Jesus, [6]so that, with one mind and one mouth, you may glorify the God and father of our Lord Jesus the Messiah.

We went to Venice last month, and marvelled again at the extraordinary achievement of the people who built that unique city many centuries ago. Just as remarkable, actually, is the achievement of those who today are propping it up and stopping it sinking into the lagoon. The whole city seems to float in its surrounding water, part river, part sea, dividing into hundreds of smaller canals as it makes its way through the ancient buildings, past curious palaces, statues, courtyards, shops and hotels ancient and modern. How do they do it?

The answer was provided when we were told the story of the great bell tower in St Mark's Square. It had stood for several hundred years, and then one day early in the twentieth century it developed some cracks and fell down. The city council agreed at once that it had to be rebuilt. This time, having discovered that the foundations had always been less than adequate, they drove hundreds of piles down into the floor of the lagoon, spreading out into a wide area so that the new bell tower is far more firmly in place than the old one ever was. Of course, you don't see these foundations. But if they weren't there, the new tower would not only fall down itself, but might damage the rest of the square as well.

Paul has hinted all through chapter 14 at the real foundations of the argument, but it's only now, as he sums it up, that he gives a full account of what they really are. Sometimes trying to navigate through the Christian life seems a bit like trying to build a city on water. There are so many things to consider, people have so many different opinions on this point and that; we so often don't even know our own minds, let alone God's, that we find ourselves floundering around and eventually taking the line of least resistance, doing whatever is easiest at the time. That way we are heading for a crash, or even a splash. What we need is firm and deep foundations for all our behaviour, individually and as a Christian family. That is what Paul now provides. No surprises, of course: the foundations are the **Messiah** himself, and the Bible as it explains the significance of what he accomplished.

When Paul quotes the Bible as he does in verse 3, he seems to us to make an effortless but puzzling move in assuming that a passage from a Psalm (here 69.9) can be taken without more ado as a reference to the Messiah. Is he simply plucking a 'proof-text' out of the air and making it do what he wants?

No, he isn't. Psalm 69 is a classic poem about the suffering of Israel in general and of the righteous one within Israel in particular. (Actually, it too has the feel of Venice about it: 'I sink in the deep mud, where there is no firm ground,' complains the writer in verse 2.) Paul has already drawn on this Psalm in 11.9–10 to interpret the events of his own day. Now he sees it as a typical statement of the plight of God's people, summed up in the plight of their ultimate representative, their anointed king. The poem works its way through the present plight of the writer, via the summoning of God's judgment against evil, to a great final outpouring of praise for God's deliverance. This was the pattern of Jesus' own life, the messianic path he was called to tread as, in his own person, he summed up the obedience of Israel to God's saving plan (see 3.21–26 and 5.12–21).

Let's just pause there and reflect, in the light of Paul's extra comment in verse 4, on the way in which the Bible is meant to function in ordinary Christian living. Paul is of course talking about what we call the 'Old Testament' (not much of the New Testament even existed when he was writing this letter). And his view of a Christian use of the Old Testament is clear: it is written for us to learn from, so that with the Bible in our hands and hearts we might have the courage to live in patience and hope. The Bible, in other words, is the earlier part of the story we ourselves are living in, explaining the roots from which we have grown.

Or, if you like, it gives us the foundation on which, despite appearances, we can build securely for the future.

Many Christians fail to learn this lesson. Some disregard the Old Testament almost entirely, supposing that it's been made redundant, or even disproved, by the coming of Christianity. (Sometimes people even quote Paul himself to back this up, with statements like 'Christ is the end of the **law**' (10.4); but Paul would have been horrified at this misinterpretation.) Other Christians, determined to take all scripture seriously, have tried to insist that the whole Old Testament, as it stands, is still valid; some have even proposed that the **Temple** in Jerusalem should be rebuilt so that the **sacrifices** can be restarted in obedience to Old Testament instruction. Others again, aware that the New Testament explicitly declares various parts of the Old to be now redundant (the sacrificial system is a case in point, as the letter to the Hebrews argues in detail), have tried to set out principles for determining which bits of the Old Testament are still 'valid' and which bits aren't.

Paul, as a good first-century Jew who had thought through his theology in the light of his belief that Jesus was and is the Messiah, would have said that this last position, though on the right lines, isn't going about it in the right way. It isn't that some parts of the Bible are valid and others aren't. Rather, the whole Old Testament forms the God-given story of how the **covenant** people were called to bring God's salvation to the good but fallen creation. This necessarily involved them, and would necessarily involve their ultimate representative, the Messiah, in terrible suffering, standing at the place where the world, and humankind in particular, was in pain with its own rebellion and failure. Now that the Messiah had come and had achieved what the whole Old Testament had been moving towards, the Bible could be read not as a puzzling story in search of an ending but as the foundation for God's great achievement in Jesus. From that point, it would become an enormous encouragement to faithful, patient Christian living. It would reinforce the belief that God would complete what he had already accomplished. Learning to read the Old Testament, in all its elements, by this rule is of course a complex task, but it is supremely worth making the effort, not just for intellectual satisfaction but, much more, for the strong sense of hope which it provides.

So how does Paul himself apply this to the Messiah and to the ongoing **life** of his people? On the basis of Psalm 69, he sets out a principle: even the Messiah was not able to 'please himself', but instead had to take on himself the insults which people were heaping on to Israel's God. This fits closely with what he says about Jesus in passages like Philippians 2.6–8 and 2 Corinthians 8.9, where Jesus humbles himself, refusing the honours which were his by right, in order to be obedient to God's saving plan. We shouldn't miss the link by which Paul joins this point with his appeal to 'the strong' (people who, like himself, knew that God had created all foods and that no food was unclean in itself, as he says in 14.14). He is saying that the self-humiliation, the renouncing of rights, which formed the path Jesus had to tread to complete his messianic work, is also the path which Christians must tread as they put that work into practice. This fits closely with the appeal he makes in 1 Corinthians 9 and Philippians 2.1–5.

Indeed, the appeal in that passage of Philippians for people to *think in the same way* as one another is echoed exactly in verse 5. This is at first strange. The whole point of the discussion from 14.1 onwards has been to address the situation of how Christians are to live alongside people who do *not* think like them, and how they must not try to force others into the position they themselves have taken up. But Paul is urging a different point. He is insisting that *all* Christians should learn to think the same *about mutual submission in accordance with the Messiah.*

That is the way to the goal he has in mind, which he will spell out more fully in the next passage, where the theological argument of the letter comes to its great conclusion. The point of it all is not simply being able to live in peace and quiet without squabbling. That would be, so to speak, simply clearing the ground of rubble. The point is to build: and what needs to be built is the common life of praise and worship. 'With one mind' and 'with one mouth' go closely together, describing that glad unanimity of praise and worship which indicates both to the watching world and to the Christians themselves that they are not worshipping a merely local deity, the projection of their own culture, but the One True God of all the world, the God now known as the father of Jesus the Messiah.

ROMANS 15.7–13

United Praise under the Messiah's Universal Rule

[7]Welcome one another, therefore, as the Messiah has welcomed you, to God's glory. [8]Let me tell you why: the Messiah became a servant of the circumcised people in order to demonstrate the truthfulness of God – that is, to confirm the promises to the patriarchs, [9]and to bring the nations to praise God for his mercy. As the Bible says:

That is why I will praise you among the nations,
and will sing to your name.

[10]And again it says,

Rejoice, you nations, with his people.

[11]And again,

Praise the Lord, all nations,
And let all the peoples sing his praise.

[12]And Isaiah says once more:

There shall be the root of Jesse,
the one who rises up to rule the nations;
the nations shall hope in him.

[13]May the God of hope fill you with all joy and peace in believing, so that you may overflow with hope by the power of the holy spirit.

The great Finnish composer Jean Sibelius brought the art of writing symphonies to a new glory. His first six were each splendid in their own way, developing the form which previous composers had used and flooding it not only with new themes but with new ways of developing and combining them. But in his Seventh Symphony he moved into a different mode again. If we listen carefully, we can trace elements of the traditional four-movement structure. The music passes through different moods that correspond in some ways to the regular pattern. But Sibelius has woven the whole thing together into a single great movement, far more tightly knit together than anything he or anyone else had attempted previously. It remains one of the most sub-lime pieces of music ever written.

This great symphony begins and ends in the key which, for many composers, has been a kind of 'home base', that of C major. (You might suppose that they regarded this key in this way because it is the easiest to play on the piano, but I think the opposite is the case: pianos were designed that way because C major was already recognized as a kind of ultimate starting and stopping point.) This is part of the great appeal of Sibelius' Seventh Symphony, providing a lasting sense of satisfaction at having worked through all the different moods and returned, full and grateful, to where we started. Something of the same sense is captured in T. S. Eliot's famous lines, in 'Little Gidding', the last of his *Four Quartets*, in which he speaks of arriving at last at the place where we began and knowing it for the first time.

Something of this same effect, I suggest, is what Paul achieves in the present passage. This is often overlooked, because many readers of Romans come to the letter with particular questions to which they find the answers in the earlier chapters and then retire exhausted, like someone listening only to the first ten minutes of Sibelius's Seventh Symphony and then, having heard a favourite tune, walking out of the concert. Romans, of course, like a great symphony, does have some obvious 'movements', and we have noted them as we have gone through. Chapters 1—4, 5—8 and 9—11 each form a single section with its own integrity, its own argument, its own great themes developed in their own way. So, too, does the section which runs from the beginning of chapter 12 to the end of the present passage (15.14 to the end of the letter function as a kind of personal conclusion). But Paul has clearly had the whole thing in mind all through, and the four main sections are stitched together with so many criss-crossing themes, so many tunes that echo previous material or anticipate what is to come, that the Sibelius analogy has considerable force at this point too.

The main thing to notice, though, is the 'key' in which Paul's argument ends as it began. In 1.1–5, Paul sets out the **gospel** which he has been commissioned to announce among all the nations. Its main content is Jesus: Jesus as the **son of David** who is also the **son of God**, Jesus who has risen from the dead, Jesus who is now the Lord of the whole world. This is his 'home base', the Christian equivalent of the musician's key of C major. Most of the great tunes of Romans have been either in this key or in another closely related to it.

Now, as the letter draws to its close, Paul works round to another stunning statement of the same theme, in the same key. Beginning in verse 9, he quotes passage after passage to show that God always intended to bring the nations of the world into equal fellowship with his chosen people, Israel. The Psalmist, celebrating the great victory which Israel's God has given him, declares that he will praise him not only in Israel but among the nations (verse 9, quoting Psalm 18.49). Moses, celebrating God's sovereign victory over, and just judgment upon, both rebellious Israel and the pagan nations, summons those nations to rejoice in this God alongside Israel (verse 10, quoting Deuteronomy 32.43 – a passage closely related to others which Paul used in chapters 9—11). He returns to the Psalms in verse 11, quoting Psalm 117.1 as a summons to all nations, not just Israel, to worship the one true God. Then, finally, he returns to his beloved Isaiah, and discovers there, in Isaiah 11.10, a statement which both fits the sequence of thought in the present passage and more or less exactly matches 1.3–4:

> There shall be the root of Jesse,
> the one who rises up to rule the nations;
> the nations shall hope in him.

Jesse was the father of King David. Isaiah is referring back to the beginning of the chapter (Isaiah 11.1), in which the **Messiah** is a fresh branch growing out of the old royal root after it had appeared to be cut down. In the original text, people might have read the next line as meaning, simply, that this new king will 'arise' in the sense of 'come to the fore' or 'emerge from among the people'. But the word in the version Paul quotes is one of the two regular ones he and other early Christians used for the **resurrection** itself.

We remind ourselves again of 1.4: Jesus was powerfully declared to be God's son, the true Messiah and the living embodiment of God himself, through the resurrection of the dead. Now here he is again, with his resurrection constituting him as the world's true Lord. The nations are to be summoned to worship him, to submit to him, and here in particular to *hope* in him. He will not simply rule them with a rod of iron, bringing God's judgment upon them. He will rule in such a way as to bring hope to the whole world, something sorely lacking then as (so often) today. In and through all of this, as we saw at the beginning of the letter, Paul is putting down a cheerful but direct challenge to the one whom most of the known world of the time, and certainly the people to whom he was writing, saw as 'the ruler of the nations'. Jesus is the reality; Caesar is simply a caricature, a sham.

This string of triumphant passages thus draws Paul's long argument to a close with a summary statement of the entire gospel and its meaning for bringing Jews and **Gentiles** together into a single family. The mutual welcome which Christians from different backgrounds must offer one another (verse 7) grows directly out of the primary narrative, the basic Christian story, which Paul here summarizes as concisely as anywhere in all his writings (verses 8 and 9). We need to expand it just a little to bring out its full flavour and its relation to the rest of the letter.

The Messiah became a servant to the **circumcised** (that is, to Israel, the ancient people of God, the physical family of Abraham). This was in order to embody and demonstrate God's truthfulness (which had been called into question by Israel's own rebellion, as in 3.1–9; Paul has not forgotten this theme, even though many of his readers ignore it!). It was, more specifically, to establish the promises God had made to Abraham, Isaac and Jacob, as we have seen in chapters 4 and 9 in particular. But the aim of those promises was never simply that Israel would be a great nation, distinct from and superior to all others. To think like that was the primal mistake which Paul sees in 'Israel according to the flesh', including his own former self. It was always so that, *through* Israel, God would call people of every nation into the one family of salvation and praise. That, he declares triumphantly, is what has now been done through Jesus the Messiah, and all that remains is for the call to go out – the summons to obedience, **faith** and above all worship.

And, just as in 1.4 Paul emphasized that God's public affirmation of Jesus in the resurrection took place by the power of the **holy spirit**, so here he invokes that same power (verse 13), the power which will surge through the little Christian community and enable it to celebrate, to live at peace, to hold firm the faith, and above all to abound in hope. Verse 13 is one of those summary verses which says so much in such a short space that it would be worth learning it by heart, mulling it over again and again, and turning it into prayer, prayer for our own churches, prayer for the worldwide church today and tomorrow, prayer for God to be glorified in the **life** of his people.

ROMANS 15.14–24

Coming to Rome at Last

[14]When I think of you, my dear family, I myself am thoroughly convinced that you are full of goodness, filled with all knowledge, and well able to give one another instruction. [15]But I have written to you very boldly at some points, calling things to your mind through the grace which God has given me [16]to enable me to be a minister of King Jesus for the nations, working in the priestly service of God's good news, so that the offering of the nations may be acceptable, sanctified in the holy spirit.

[17]This is the confidence I have in King Jesus, and in God's own presence. [18]Far be it from me, you see, to speak about anything except what the Messiah has accomplished through me for the obedience of the nations, in word and deed, [19]in the power of signs and wonders, in the power of God's spirit. I have completed announcing the good news of the Messiah from Jerusalem round as far as Illyricum. [20]My driving ambition has been to announce the good news in places where the Messiah has not been named,

so that I can avoid building on anyone else's foundation. [21]Instead, as the Bible says,

People who hadn't been told about him will hear;
People who hadn't heard will understand.

[22]That's why I have faced so many obstacles to stop me coming to you. [23]But now, finding myself with no more work in these regions, I have a great longing to come to you now at last after so many years, [24]and so to make my way to Spain. You see, I'm hoping to see you as I pass through, and to be sent on my way there by you, once I have been refreshed by you for a while.

I mentioned earlier in this book how, when my family and I first moved to North America, we were struck again and again at the thought of what the pioneers had achieved in such very recent history. They had navigated uncharted rivers, climbed mountains not even named until that point, carved roads through dense forests and taken whole wagon trains across seemingly unending plains, through steep passes, on and on for thousands of miles. At each point they had faced dangers they couldn't foresee, tried to grow crops without knowing if the soil was right, endured extremes of heat and cold, and had to rely on their wits and their sheer brute strength to see them through. In that context, the very word 'pioneer' has a ring, an excitement, a sense of drama and courageous accomplishment.

Paul had understood from the very beginning that his special vocation had been to pioneer the **gospel** in places where it had never been heard. Again and again he had found himself standing in synagogues and market-places, in private houses and public halls, before magistrates and rulers and ordinary folk in towns and villages. He was telling them the extraordinary news that there was one true God rather than the multiplicity of pagan deities, that this one true God had made the world, still loved it, and was bringing it justice and hope, and that this God, to fulfil this plan, had sent his own son, his own second self, to suffer the fate of a rebel against the empire and now to be enthroned as the world's true Lord. To say that he has written boldly at some points in the letter (verse 15) is to say, why change the habit of a lifetime? Paul had been speaking and acting boldly ever since he had met the risen Jesus on the road to Damascus.

According to verse 16, he saw this work – another bold move, this – as being like a **priest** in the **Temple**. Only instead of the animals to be offered in **sacrifice**, he was bringing the **Gentile** nations themselves, in their new-found **faith** and obedience, as an offering to the one true God, made holy not by who they were in themselves but by the work of the **holy spirit** (verse 16). No pagan had ever imagined such a thing happening. No Jew had ever thought of it like that, let alone attempted it. That was what it was like being a pioneer.

But Paul was conscious that there were other **apostles**. There were other missionaries who had gone around also announcing the **good news** of Jesus. Some of them had visited churches which he himself had founded, and that had sometimes caused problems, as we see in the two letters to Corinth. Paul was naturally anxious in case he should do to other pioneers what others had done to him. This was so particularly as he planned his visit to Rome.

The situation there was complicated because of the movement of people, particularly those Jewish Christians who had left Rome some years previously and had now returned. Some of them had been members of churches Paul had founded, notably Prisca and Aquila, whom we shall meet in 16.3–4 and who had actually worked alongside Paul as trusted friends and colleagues. Some of them, though, were native Roman Christians who had embraced the faith when it had been proclaimed by . . . who? Tradition says Peter, though we have no firm evidence on the point. Some people think Christianity arrived in the imperial capital simply through the travelling witness of ordinary Christians whose names are now unknown. But it may be that Paul is aware of the work of Peter in Rome, so that even though the church now contains several people who had come to faith through his own work before moving there, he knows it is wise to tread carefully.

That is why he writes somewhat obliquely in verses 18 and 20. It's hard to bring out, in translation, just how cryptic verse 18 sounds in Greek: it comes out more or less as, 'For I will not dare to say anything of what the **Messiah** has not accomplished through me for the obedience of the nations in word and deed.' As so often, a double negative can be heard in various ways, and Paul is pretty clearly acknowledging, with tactful reticence, that others have been at work as well. He sketches out his own qualifications without presuming to say a word about what anyone else has done.

He is therefore coming to Rome, not to build on a foundation someone else has laid (he uses the same image in 1 Corinthians 3.10–17, where it's clear he sees his own vocation as a primary founder, not a secondary builder), but to do fresh work for the gospel. That is his basic task, and as elsewhere (e.g. 10.16) he understands it in the light of scripture, particularly those passages such as Isaiah 52.15, which he quotes in verse 21, which speak of the Suffering Servant and of those who announce his work to the world.

At this point we need to draw in 1.10–13. There he is careful not to claim that he is coming in order to do primary evangelism, and suggests instead that the visit will be an occasion for mutual encouragement. There would still, of course, be plenty of room in Rome for pioneer evangelism: it was an enormous city by ancient standards, with at least a million inhabitants, and with probably no more than a hundred or so Christians in the city one could hardly suppose that there was no more room for fresh work. But Paul is anxious not to give the wrong impression. This is almost certainly why he speaks so eagerly about going on to Spain.

Going to Spain is a whole new idea at this point in the letter. Nothing elsewhere in Paul, or indeed in Acts, prepares us for this ambition. But it is consistent with everything we know of Paul. He has longed to name Jesus as Messiah and Lord right around the Gentile world, the Roman world; and from what he would have known of geography, Spain would represent the western limits of the world (just as St Patrick thought he had got to the north-western limits of the world when he went to Ireland). Spain had been a major centre of Roman influence for centuries by this time, and there is evidence for first-century Jewish communities there as virtually everywhere else in the empire. Paul was longing to do there what he had done everywhere else.

This helps us to understand something vital about why Paul wrote Romans. Up to now, his base of operations, his 'home church' insofar as he had one by this stage, was Antioch, near the coast of north-west Syria. But Paul had faced serious difficulties there, as we know from Galatians 2.11–14, precisely on the point of how the gospel worked its way out in the common life of the church where Jews and Gentiles were called together in a single faith and family. Perhaps this is part at least of what Paul has been eager to do in this letter: to sketch out more fully the big picture of God's purposes, stressing particularly the unity of the Messiah's family and the way in which this works out both for Jews and Gentiles, in order now to bring the Roman Christians on board as his mission partners, perhaps even as his new home church, for his onward journeys.

Did Paul ever get to Spain? There is no evidence whatever that he did. But his desire to do so, and the fact that he wrote Romans as part of the preparation for such a trip, points out an extremely important lesson for us all. Perhaps God sometimes allows us to dream dreams of what he wants us to do, not necessarily so that we can fulfil all of them – that might just make us proud and self-satisfied – but so that we will take the first steps towards fulfilling them.

And perhaps those first steps (as they appear to us) are in fact the key things that God *actually* wants us to do. Paul may not have got to Spain. That didn't matter; the gospel got there fairly soon anyway. What mattered then, and has mattered enormously in the whole history of the church, is that, as part of his plan to go to Spain, he wrote Romans. We should never underestimate what God will do through things which we see as small steps to a larger end.

ROMANS 15.25–33

Aid for Jerusalem

²⁵Now, though, I am going to Jerusalem with money for God's people there. ²⁶Macedonia and Achaea, you see, have happily decided to enter into partnership with the poor believers in Jerusalem. ²⁷They were eager to do this, and indeed they owe them a debt. If the nations have shared in the Jews' spiritual blessings, it is right and proper that they should minister to their earthly needs. ²⁸So when I have completed this, and tied up all the loose ends, I will come via you to Spain. ²⁹And I know that when I come to you I shall come with the full blessing of the Messiah.

³⁰I urge you, my dear family, through our Lord Jesus the Messiah and through the love of the spirit: fight the battle for me in your prayers to God on my behalf, ³¹so that I may be rescued from the unbelievers in Judaea, and so that my service for Jerusalem may be welcomed gladly by God's people. ³²If this happens, I will come to you in joy, through the will of God, and be refreshed by being with you. ³³May the God of peace be with you all. Amen.

I have now translated most of the New Testament for this present series, and I've discovered one or two interesting things as I've done so. The hardest Greek I have so far faced, without a doubt, is in one particular section of 2 Corinthians, namely chapters 8 and 9. I think I know the reason. That is where Paul talks, at length, about money.

Anyone who has had anything to do with church finances will understand why. We all know that money matters, but few of us like talking about it. There are some cultures in which it seems easier to do than in others, and there are some people who seem to have overcome their inhibitions and to be able to say what needs to be said. But I sense in Paul what I see in myself and in a great many others: a reluctance even to raise the topic at all, and then a sense of nervousness in what we say, lest at any point we should be misunderstood.

This is so despite the fact that Paul is very clear that he is not raising money, and has never raised money, for himself. As he explains in 1 Corinthians 9, he has operated a settled principle of working with his own hands to support himself so that no church can claim to have 'bought' him or his **message**. This practice formed a striking contrast with that of the many popular philosophers who roamed the ancient world, offering their teaching only to those who would pay. Equally, Paul stresses – at the risk of being called inconsistent! – that, despite his example, which was set for other purposes, the church has a definite obligation to pay those who work for the **gospel**, including special rates for those who work hard at preaching and teaching (1 Corinthians 9.7–14; Galatians 6.6–10; 1 Timothy 5.17). But in the collection to which he refers here and elsewhere, the money was emphatically not for himself or his fellow-workers. It was for someone else.

It was, specifically, for the Christians in Judaea. We thereby meet a triple irony, worth reflecting on carefully.

First, one of the reasons why the church in Judaea was poor seems to be that in their first flush of enthusiasm for the gospel they had done what some other renewal movements of their day had done. They had pooled their property, selling farms and fields and putting the money into common possession. But now, following a famine, and no doubt facing hostility from their own fellow Judaeans who rejected the gospel and resented their allegiance to it, they were in dire need. Meanwhile Paul, as part of his regular Christian teaching, had been instructing **Gentile** communities not to sell up and have a common purse, but to look after one another's physical and financial needs from within communities where, it was assumed, some would continue to own houses and businesses and be in a position to help others. The same end was in view, namely that none should be in want. The same theology underlay both patterns, namely the self-giving of God in Jesus as the pattern and model. But the practice was different. Now Paul, with his way of doing things, was in a position to help the churches in Judaea, whose early experiment seems to have ended in failure, perhaps through no fault of their own.

Second, it was from Judaea that there had come the settled and sustained Christian opposition to Paul and his gospel which had dogged his footsteps from the early days in Galatia. We do not know who had initiated this. Paul speaks of 'certain people coming from James' (Galatians 2.12), but he seems to imply that James himself, the leader of the Jerusalem church, was not to be blamed for what they did. How easy it would have been at this point for Paul to turn his back on them, to work with and for only those who agreed with 'the gospel' as he saw it and preached it – the gospel according to which the Gentiles were fellow heirs, on equal terms with Jewish believers. But it is precisely these people, the source of the opposition to his work, for whom Paul is now undertaking a difficult and dangerous mission. (We, who rely on electronic bank transfers and international money orders, need to pause and reflect on how Paul and his travelling companions, in the days before even paper banknotes had been invented, would have gone about safely, on roads and in boats, staying in wayside inns, with large sums of money about their persons.) There is a serious and urgent lesson there for those who are tempted to use financial muscle to exercise theological influence within the church. At the core of the gospel is God's generous love for those who were not only undeserving but also in active opposition (Romans 5.10). Even if we think we are correct in seeing certain others as in the wrong (we should, of course, always beware of our own bias), they might just be the very people we ought to be helping.

Third, the two short paragraphs in this passage (verses 25–29 and 30–33) are therefore in something of a tension. On the one hand, Paul is eager to demonstrate that Jewish Christians and Gentile Christians belong in the same family. The Gentiles have shared in the spiritual blessings of Israel, and now they must repay in practical terms (verse 27). The collection therefore does in severely practical terms what the doctrine of **justification** by **faith** does in theological terms. It insists to Gentile Christians that their own roots are in Israel itself (11.11–24); it insists to Jewish Christians that their **Messiah** is the one Lord of Gentiles as well (3.27–30; 9.5; 10.12).

But just for that reason, on the other hand, Paul expects opposition – from two quarters. First, there will be Jewish non-Christians, who will bitterly resent his coming to Jerusalem. They will see him as a traitor, a blasphemer, someone who has led Jewish people astray and destroyed the grip of the **law** of Moses on their lives. Second, there will be many of the Jewish Christians themselves, who for the reasons mentioned a moment ago may well find it difficult to accept money raised from non-Jewish sources.

It is, they may think, 'tainted'. Who knows by what means those Gentiles acquired it? Were they involved in idolatry? Were they doing business with others who were?

For that reason Paul urges the Roman Christians to pray for him. He has a clear sense of vocation to come to Rome, but there are major battles up ahead before he can get there. Indeed, he is setting off in the other direction altogether, going east to Jerusalem before he goes west again to Rome. As we know from Acts, the trip would indeed be a near-disaster, involving riots, beatings and trials, two years of imprisonment, a complex sea voyage and a shipwreck. We are invited, looking on, to join both in gratitude to God for all that Paul accomplished and in urgent prayer for those who preach the gospel in our own day, especially where it crosses important cultural boundaries. Not only money, but power and the deepest sense of human identity, are challenged by the message which declares that there is one God and that the crucified and risen Jesus is his son, the world's true Lord.

ROMANS 16.1–16

Commending Phoebe, Greeting Friends

[1]Let me introduce to you our sister Phoebe. She is a deacon in the church at Cenchreae. [2]I want you to welcome her in the Lord, as is proper for one of God's people. Please give her whatever practical assistance she may need from you. She has been a benefactor to many people, myself included.

[3]Greet Prisca and Aquila, my fellow-workers in King Jesus. [4]They put their lives on the line for me. It isn't only me, but all the Gentile churches, that owe them a debt of gratitude. [5]Greet the church in their house as well.

Greet my dear Epainetus; he was the first sign of the Messiah's harvest in Asia. [6]Greet Mary, who has worked hard for you. [7]Greet Andronicus and Junia, my relatives and fellow prisoners, who are well known among the apostles, and who were in the Messiah before I was. [8]Greet Ampliatus, my dear friend in the Lord. [9]Greet Urbanus, our fellow-worker in the Messiah, and my dear Stachys. [10]Greet Apelles, who has proved his worth in the Messiah. Greet the people from the Aristobulus household.

[11]Greet my relative Herodion. Greet those in the Lord who belong to the household of Narcissus. [12]Greet Tryphaena and Tryphosa, who have worked hard in the Lord. Greet dear Persis, who has done a great deal of work in the Lord. [13]Greet Rufus, one of the Lord's chosen, and also his mother – my mother too, in effect! [14]Greet Asyncritus, Phlegon, Hermes, Patrobas, Hermas and the family with them.

[15]Greet Philologus and Julia, Nereus and his sister, Olympas, and all God's people who are with them. [16]Greet one another with a holy kiss. All the Messiah's churches send you greetings.

A farmer in the English Midlands was ploughing a field when the plough struck a solid object. Thinking it was a large rock, he stopped to move it. But it wasn't a rock. It was an ancient chest, dating (so the museum told him when he took it there) to Anglo-Saxon times. And it was full of all kinds of small objects. How it got there, and why it came to the surface at that point, history so far doesn't relate.

A discovery like that leaves us both fascinated and frustrated. Who owned it? What are these little objects, like long pins with a hook on the end? Is this a primitive mirror, and how does it relate to other similar objects found elsewhere? Whose is the picture carved into that goblet? Might it have been a portrait of the owner or his wife? We are in touch with the world of many centuries ago; we have a sense of being near to knowing quite a lot; and yet we are still a long way from uncovering the innermost secrets.

That is exactly how I feel when I read Romans 16. Here are no fewer than *twenty-four* names of Christians in Rome, plus one other (Rufus' mother) who isn't named; and we know almost nothing about any of them. (If you're counting the names, note that two of the people mentioned in this list, Aristobulus and Narcissus, were not themselves Christians, so far as we know, but rather the heads of great houses in Rome in which some of the Christians lived. Narcissus, in fact, had been a favourite of the Emperor Claudius, and had committed suicide after Claudius' death in AD 54; clearly his household had not dispersed.) In one or two cases the people concerned are mentioned elsewhere in the New Testament: Prisca (or 'Priscilla', presumably a familiar form of the same name) and Aquila in Acts 18, Rufus (if it's the same one) in Mark 15.21. There are so many Marys in the **gospel** story, and the name was so frequent among ancient Jews, that we can't tell if the Mary in verse 6 is one we know from elsewhere, but my guess is that she isn't.

What can we learn from this teasing list of greetings, then? Plenty of things. First, of course, the strong sense of love and affection which bound Paul to Christians from various backgrounds in the imperial capital, and which he longed to see at work among them as well. The only other letter which comes close to Romans in the length of the greetings list is Colossians, significantly the only other one which is written to a church Paul had not at that stage visited himself. Clearly the greetings were more than a formality. Paul intended thereby to embrace all these people within a sense of mutual ministry and support.

Anyone who has ever had to make a speech of thanks or greeting to even a smallish gathering knows very well that once you start listing people you'd better include everyone you can think of. Nobody likes to be the one left out. For this reason we can be reasonably sure – assuming Paul has good information about Rome, which his friendship with Prisca and Aquila, and his location in or near Corinth when writing this letter, on easy trade and postal routes to Rome, more or less guaranteed – that he has included at least a mention of each of the house churches, the local fellowship gatherings, within Rome. There are five in all: the church that meets with Prisca and Aquila, the households of Aristobulus and of Narcissus, the people with Asyncritus and the others in verse 14, and those with Philologus and the others in verse 15. There are several other Christians whose particular grouping Paul does not mention. This gives us an idea of the spread of Christianity in Rome. It may be, like the scholars studying the contents of the newly discovered chest, that further work on ancient documents and archaeological sites will reveal more about how many Christians were in Rome altogether and what sort of people they were. If we were to guess at a maximum of twenty for each group of Christians, that would still only give us a hundred, plus a few stray names whose allegiance we do not know. It may well have been fewer.

Part of Paul's point in addressing the Christians in this way, group by group, seems to be hidden in what he invites them to do in verse 16: to greet one another with a holy kiss. The 'kiss of peace' became a key feature of Christian liturgy very early on. This was not intended to replace normal expressions of affection; as today in many parts of the Middle East and elsewhere, but unlike the more reserved modern Western world, a kiss on both cheeks is a normal greeting between men as well as women. Rather, it was meant to show, within the context of shared worship, that one belonged to the same family, the family redefined in and around the **Messiah**. It was both a reminder of, and perhaps a means of, that unity for which Paul so longed, as we saw in chapters 14, 15 and elsewhere.

Within that, there are several names which strike us as interesting in their own right. We note, not least, the importance of the women in the list. Paul names them as fellow-workers, without any sense that they hold a secondary position to the men. One of them, Junia in verse 7, is an **apostle**: the phrase 'well known among the apostles' doesn't mean that the apostles know her and Andronicus (probably wife and husband), but that they *are* apostles, that is, they were among those who saw the risen Lord. She has the same status as all the other apostles, including Paul himself. Don't be put off by some translations which call her 'Junias', as if she were a man. There is no reason for this except the anxiety of some about recognizing that women could be apostles too.

And of course, heading the chapter, is a Christian not in Rome but in Cenchreae, where Paul has been staying. Cenchreae was the eastern port of Corinth, the place from which Paul could expect to get a boat going anywhere in the Aegean sea or further east. There is already a church there; in our own day the land at that point has slipped into the sea, and some years ago I had the excitement of swimming underwater to see the site for myself. Anyway, Phoebe is a deacon in this church, holding an office whose precise significance remains a matter of debate (it was probably a junior role, below those who were variously called 'elders' or 'overseers') but which clearly involved some responsibility.

Phoebe has, says Paul, been a *benefactor* to himself and many others (verse 2). That doesn't just mean that she has helped him out with hospitality, though that may have been so as well. It means that she belongs in that class of people, vital for the health of ancient societies, who put their private means at public disposal. To be called a 'benefactor' was a great honour. Indeed, the emperor himself claimed to be the state's supreme benefactor. Phoebe was clearly a person of substance and leadership. She was almost certainly going to Rome on business on her own account, and it is a matter of great significance that it is to her that Paul entrusts the delivery of this, his fullest and most remarkable letter.

ROMANS 16.17–23

Warnings and Greetings

[17]I urge you, my dear family, to watch out for those who cause divisions and problems, contrary to the teaching you learned. Avoid them. [18]People like that are serving their own appetites instead of our Lord the Messiah. They deceive the hearts of simple-minded people with their smooth and flattering speech. [19]Your obedience, you see, is well known to all, and so I am rejoicing over you. But I want you to be wise when it comes to good, and innocent when it comes to evil. [20]The God of peace will quickly crush the satan under your feet. May the grace of our Lord Jesus be with you.

[21]Timothy, my fellow-worker, sends you greetings, as do Lucius, Jason and Sosipater, my relatives. [22]I, Tertius,

the scribe for this letter, greet you in the Lord. ²³Gaius, who is host to me and the whole church, sends you greetings. Erastus the city treasurer sends you greetings, as does another brother, Quartus.

It had been a difficult meeting. Several complex issues had been on the table, some of them involving delicate political issues, others involving money. It was right at the end of a busy university term, and everyone was tired and inclined to be scratchy and cross. Finally the debates were finished, the votes were taken, and we all retired for a cup of tea. On the way out of the room one of my colleagues, a distinguished historian, turned to me.

'I know our Lord told us', he said, 'to be wise as serpents and innocent as doves. But, being busy men, some of us find it advisable to *specialize*.'

No prizes for guessing which side the specialization tended to fall on.

This is one of those passages (there are actually several others within the last five chapters of this letter) where we may detect in the way Paul says things a brief flash at least of memory of words of Jesus. Here in verse 19 we may be right to hear an echo of that famous saying of Jesus in Matthew 10.16 about the doves and the serpents – which may be part of the reason why he then declares that God will soon crush **the satan**, the old serpent itself, underfoot. (This looks like an allusion to Genesis 3.15: as before in this letter, Paul has the story of Adam and Eve as the backdrop to what he is saying.)

In particular, he wants the church to grow up and learn how to understand, in love and good sense, that there is an ever-present danger of false teaching in the church.

Coupled with this there is, of course, an ever-present danger that people will imagine false teaching where there is none, or will label as 'false teaching' something which just happens not to coincide with the particular way they are used to hearing things said. Recognizing these wrinkles and possibilities is part of learning to be both wise and innocent. But noting the dangers of wrong analysis doesn't mean there isn't after all such a thing as false teaching. There is, and it matters.

The trouble is, of course, that false teachers seldom give themselves away easily. What they say sounds clear, convincing and attractive – as does a great deal of good and wholesome teaching. Many Christians, for good reasons, like to believe what they are taught and to take it on board with humility and trust, and so are easy prey for those who have subtly different ideas and a clever way of putting them across. But Paul sees that the church is caught in the crossfire of spiritual warfare. It isn't a matter of simply getting one's doctrine correct out of a sense of intellectual pride. There is a battle raging for the redemption and renewal of the world and of individual people, and the church is up against the powers of darkness. Paul doesn't spell this out in detail here the way he does in Ephesians 6.11–20, but verse 20 indicates surely enough that this is how he sees things. What they need is both the assurance that victory will be theirs and the promise and prayer of fresh grace to be with them in every need.

The touchstone for detecting false teaching is that it is 'contrary to the teaching you learned'. This of course depends on having healthy initial teaching! The reason Paul can be sure of this in the case of the Roman church is not simply because some of the Christians there were his own converts, but because he and all the other early **apostles** had an agreed standard to which they were all signed up. Paul quotes it in 1 Corinthians 15.3–8 (though the last verse looks like his own addition). It is the story of the **Messiah**'s death and **resurrection** as the fulfilment of Israel's scriptures. There are other early teachings, too, which he assumes that all Christians will know, as we see for instance in Romans 6.17 and 1 Corinthians 11.23–26. Paul assumes – to repeat something we said when talking about chapter 14 – that *not* all ideas and teachings which claim to be Christian are to be thought of as allowable options, as 'matters of indifference' which some want to believe and follow while others want to reject them. Part of that wisdom and innocence which he longs to see consists precisely in learning which things are 'indifferent' and which are vital and non-negotiable.

The false teachers, he says, are not serving Jesus himself, but rather pandering to their own appetites – literally, to their bellies (verse 18). It's not clear exactly who Paul has in mind, but the danger is ever present, particularly for those churches (always a minority within world Christianity) where there is plenty of money and the leaders are tempted to earn just a bit more by saying what certain people want to hear and avoiding topics they know will be unpopular.

As he often does, Paul includes greetings from those fellow-workers who happen to be with him, notably here his faithful friend and colleague Timothy. For the only time in his writings, he allows the **scribe** who has been taking down his dictation to add his own name to the list. One can only assume that, after keeping pace with Paul throughout Romans, Tertius reckoned he was entitled to his own small claim to fame! Some have identified the Gaius in verse 23 with the Gaius in 1 Corinthians 1.14, though it was a common name and the other one lived in Corinth, not Cenchreae. Erastus, the city treasurer, is known from an ancient inscription, and his presence here reminds us that already, within the first generation, some of the very early Christians were occupying positions of civic responsibility.

These outgoing greetings, like the list of Christians in Rome, gives us once more a flavour of what it must have felt like to be an early Christian. They were part of a tiny but exhilarating movement. They believed that the one true God had done a drastically new thing, in fulfilment of his ancient promises, and that the world was a different place as a result. They were living in God's new world. There were all kinds of dangers and challenges; but their Christian fellowship itself reminded them day by day that they were part of a family whose love and **faith** and hope would win the day. Those who follow in their footsteps nearly twenty centuries later could learn a lot from their courage and daring, and their attractive blend of wisdom and innocence.

ROMANS 16.25–27

Final Blessing

[25]Now to him who is able to strengthen you according to my gospel, the proclamation of Jesus the Messiah, in accordance with the unveiling of the mystery kept hidden for long ages [26]but now revealed and made known through the prophetic writings, according to the command of the eternal God,

for the obedience of faith among all the nations – [27]to the only wise God, through Jesus the Messiah, to whom be glory to the coming ages! Amen.

I watched as the children played in the swimming pool. The water was about four feet deep. Three of them stood side by side, with linked arms. Then they squatted down, with only their noses above water, and two others climbed on to their shoulders. Then a younger boy scrambled up on to *their* shoulders. Then, slowly but surely, the three at the bottom stood up, until the whole pyramid was nearly, very nearly, standing proudly upright.

At that moment two other children, seeing the fun, came to join in. Despite shouts of warning from some of those already involved, they tried to get in on the act, scrabbling and clutching and trying to join the little one up on the top. The whole pyramid began to wobble, and suddenly they all toppled over with legs and arms going in every direction and the most enormous splash I had ever seen in the pool.

That is, more or less, what has happened with the last sentence of this great letter. I think, actually, that Paul probably intended it this way. If he didn't – if, in other words, it just came out like that in his dictation and he didn't bother to correct it – I think he was happy with it, happy to make a final splash even though the construction of the sentence eventually gets top-heavy and falls over with legs and arms (extra phrases and clauses tagged in here and there) all over the place. Let's look at it and see how the pyramid was at least designed to work before the extra bits were added. (Talking of adding extra bits, in some early copies of this letter a scribe added an extra closing greeting which is officially labelled as verse 24. Hardly anyone now thinks Paul wrote this verse, so it's normally missed out.)

The bottom row of the pyramid is meant to say: 'To God be the glory for ever!' This divides up into three sections, closely linked. First, God is described in terms of what he can do for the Christians in Rome (for all Christians, of course, but Paul wants this church to know this in particular): he can give them strength through the **gospel**. Second, what has happened in the gospel is the fulfilment of the age-old story of God, Israel and the world. Third, this gospel has been spread around the world to bring about the obedience of **faith**. So far, so good.

Standing on the shoulders of these basic points are two more. First, the gospel has been made known through the prophetic writings: Paul may have in mind the Old Testament scriptures, or he may even be referring to some early Christian texts. Second, this has come about because of the command of God, the eternal one. Paul is clearly heaping up phrases which echo, or refer back to, entire sections of the letter that is now drawing rapidly to its close. So much of what he has been writing about has been to do with the way in which the long narrative of Israel has come to fulfilment and fruition in Jesus the **Messiah**, and with the way in which God himself, at work in and through Jesus, is now still at work through the announcement of the gospel.

What Paul then puts on top of the pyramid looks as though it's going to be: 'To the only wise God be glory for ever.' But then, like the extra child at the last minute, he realizes that he can hardly bring this letter of all letters to a conclusion without Jesus being in the very middle of it. So he adds one more phrase, which makes the whole sentence fall over, grammatically speaking, with a great splash: 'To the only wise God . . . *through Jesus the Messiah* . . . to whom be glory to the coming ages!'

Was the glory going to God, or to Jesus? Does it matter? Paul would certainly have said, 'No, it doesn't'. Throughout this letter we have seen that the living God has revealed himself in, as and through Jesus. Jesus dies as the personal expression of God's love; Paul draws on the messianic language of '**son of God**' as a way of expressing this close identity while still allowing for what later theologians would speak of as differentiation within the persons of the Trinity. Jesus is both Israel's Messiah according to the flesh and also 'God over all, blessed for ever'. Paul takes Old Testament passages which clearly refer to 'the Lord', meaning YHWH, the God of Israel, and transfers them so that they now refer to Jesus. What theologians call a 'high Christology' – a view of Jesus which sees him as fully and completely divine as well as fully and completely human – doesn't have to wait for later centuries and writers. It is already fully present in Paul, not least in this, his greatest letter.

In particular, we note that Paul refers in the closing phrases to God as 'the only wise God'. There were many other claims to wisdom in the ancient world. There were many other gods who offered insight, of a sort and at a cost. There were plenty of teachings about how to live, how to think, what to believe, how to pray. But Paul believes – and the powerful gospel of Jesus bears him out – that there is only one God who is truly wise. He is the creator. He understands how the whole world works, what humans are and how they think, where they go wrong and how they can be put to rights, and how, when that happens, the whole of creation will dance for joy at its new-found freedom. This is the hidden wisdom which formed the secret plan, the plan now unveiled in the gospel, the gospel which now evokes as its proper response 'the obedience of faith' (as in 1.5), the faith which is open to the whole world. When you see the end from the beginning in this way; when you understand Romans in its grand sweep of thought as well as its smaller, dense and deliciously chewy arguments; when you glimpse even a little of what Paul has glimpsed of the wisdom, love, grace, power and glory of the eternal God revealed in Jesus the Messiah – then you, too, will want to join him in piling up all the glory and praise and love and adoration you can muster. And you won't care how big a splash you make as you do so.

GLOSSARY

age to come, *see* **present age**

apostle, disciple, the Twelve

'Apostle' means 'one who is sent'. It could be used of an ambassador or official delegate. In the New Testament it is sometimes used specifically of Jesus' inner circle of twelve; but Paul sees not only himself but several others outside the Twelve as 'apostles', the criterion being whether the person had personally seen the risen Jesus. Jesus' own choice of twelve close associates symbolized his plan to renew God's people, Israel; after the death of Judas Iscariot (Matthew 27.5; Acts 1.18), Matthias was chosen by lot to take his place, preserving the symbolic meaning. During Jesus' lifetime they, and many other followers, were seen as his 'disciples', which means 'pupils' or 'apprentices'.

baptism

Literally, 'plunging' people into water. From within a wider Jewish tradition of ritual washings and bathings, **John the Baptist** undertook a vocation of baptizing people in the Jordan, not as one ritual among others but as a unique moment of **repentance**, preparing them for the coming of the **kingdom of God**. Jesus himself was baptized by John, identifying himself with this renewal movement and developing it in his own way. His followers in turn baptized others. After his **resurrection**, and the sending of the **holy spirit**, baptism became the normal sign and means of entry into the community of Jesus' people. As early as Paul it was aligned both with the **Exodus** from Egypt (1 Corinthians 10.2) and with Jesus' death and resurrection (Romans 6.2–11).

Christ, *see* **Messiah**

circumcision, circumcised

The cutting off of the foreskin. Male circumcision was a major mark of identity for Jews, following its initial commandment to Abraham (Genesis 17), reinforced by Joshua (Joshua 5.2–9). Other peoples, e.g. the Egyptians, also circumcised male children. A line of thought from Deuteronomy (e.g. 30.6), through Jeremiah (e.g. 31.33), to the **Dead Sea Scrolls** and the New Testament (e.g. Romans 2.29) speaks of 'circumcision of the heart' as God's real desire, by which one may become inwardly what the male Jew is outwardly, that is, marked out as part of God's people. At periods of Jewish assimilation into the surrounding culture, some Jews tried to remove the marks of circumcision (e.g. 1 Maccabees 1.11–15).

covenant

At the heart of Jewish belief is the conviction that the one God, YHWH, who had made the whole world, had called Abraham and his family to belong to him in a special way. The promises God made to Abraham and his family, and the requirements that were laid on them as a result, came to be seen in terms either of the agreement that a king would make with a subject people, or sometimes of the marriage bond between husband and wife. One regular way of describing this relationship was 'covenant', which can thus include both promise and **law**. The covenant was renewed at Mount Sinai with the giving of the **Torah**; in Deuteronomy before the entry to the promised land; and, in a more focused way, with **David** (e.g. Psalm 89). Jeremiah 31 promised that after the punishment of **exile** God would make a 'new covenant' with his people, forgiving them and binding them to him more intimately. Jesus believed that this was coming true through his **kingdom** proclamation and his death and **resurrection**. The early Christians developed these ideas in various ways, believing that in Jesus the promises had at last been fulfilled.

David, *see* son of David

146

Dead Sea Scrolls

A collection of texts, some in remarkably good repair, some extremely fragmentary, found in the late 1940s around Qumran (near the northeast corner of the Dead Sea), and virtually all now edited, translated and in the public domain. They formed all or part of the library of a strict monastic group, most likely Essenes, founded in the mid-second century BC and lasting until the Jewish–Roman war of 66–70. The scrolls include the earliest existing manuscripts of the Hebrew and Aramaic scriptures, and several other important documents of community regulations, scriptural exegesis, hymns, wisdom writings, and other literature. They shed a flood of light on one small segment within the Judaism of Jesus' day, helping us to understand how some Jews at least were thinking, praying and reading scripture. Despite attempts to prove the contrary, they make no reference to **John the Baptist**, Jesus, Paul, James or early Christianity in general.

demons, *see* **the satan**

disciple, *see* **apostle**

Essenes, *see* **Dead Sea Scrolls**

eternal life, *see* **present age**

eucharist

The meal in which the earliest Christians, and Christians ever since, obeyed Jesus' command to 'do this in remembrance of him' at the Last Supper (Luke 22.19; 1 Corinthians 11.23–26). The word 'eucharist' itself comes from the Greek for 'thanksgiving'; it means, basically, 'the thank-you meal', and looks back to the many times when Jesus took bread, gave thanks for it, broke it, and gave it to people (e.g. Luke 24.30; John 6.11). Other early phrases for the same meal are 'the Lord's supper' (1 Corinthians 11.20) and 'the breaking of bread' (Acts 2.42). Later it came to be called 'the Mass' (from the Latin word at the end of the service, meaning 'sent out') and 'Holy

Communion' (Paul speaks of 'sharing' or 'communion' in the body and blood of Christ). Later theological controversies about the precise meaning of the various actions and elements of the meal should not obscure its centrality in earliest Christian living and its continuing vital importance today.

exile

Deuteronomy (29—30) warned that if Israel disobeyed YHWH, he would send his people into exile, but that if they then repented he would bring them back. When the Babylonians sacked Jerusalem and took the people into exile, prophets such as Jeremiah interpreted this as the fulfilment of this prophecy, and made further promises about how long exile would last (70 years, according to Jeremiah 25.12; 29.10). Sure enough, exiles began to return in the late sixth century (Ezra 1.1). However, the post-exilic period was largely a disappointment, since the people were still enslaved to foreigners (Nehemiah 9.36); and at the height of persecution by the Syrians, Daniel 9.2, 24 spoke of the 'real' exile lasting not for 70 years but for 70 *weeks* of years, i.e. 490 years. Longing for the real 'return from exile', when the prophecies of Isaiah, Jeremiah, etc. would be fulfilled, and redemption from pagan oppression accomplished, continued to characterize many Jewish movements, and was a major theme in Jesus' proclamation and his summons to **repentance**.

Exodus

The Exodus from Egypt took place, according to the book of that name, under the leadership of Moses, after long years in which the Israelites had been enslaved there. (According to Genesis 15.13f., this was itself part of God's covenanted promise to Abraham.) It demonstrated, to them and to Pharaoh, King of Egypt, that Israel was God's special child (Exodus 4.22). They then wandered through the Sinai wilderness for 40 years, led by God in a pillar of cloud and fire; early on in this time they were given the **Torah** on Mount Sinai itself. Finally, after the death of Moses and under the leadership of Joshua, they crossed the Jordan and entered, and eventually conquered, the promised land of Canaan. This event, commemorated annually in Passover and other Jewish festivals, gave the Israelites not only a powerful memory of what had made them a people, but also a particular shape and content to their faith in YHWH as not only creator but also redeemer; and in subsequent enslavements, particularly the **exile**, they looked for a further redemption which would be, in effect, a new Exodus. Probably no other past event so dominated the imagination of first-century Jews; among them the early Christians, following the lead of Jesus himself, continually referred back to the Exodus to give meaning and shape to their own critical events, most particularly Jesus' death and **resurrection**.

faith

Faith in the New Testament covers a wide area of human trust and trustworthiness, merging into love at one end of the scale and loyalty at the other. Within Jewish and Christian thinking faith in God also includes *belief*, accepting certain things as true about God, and what he has done in the world (e.g. bringing Israel out of Egypt; raising Jesus from the dead). For Jesus, 'faith' often seems to mean 'recognizing that God is decisively at work to bring the **kingdom** through Jesus'. For Paul, 'faith' is both the specific belief that Jesus is Lord and that God raised him from the dead (Romans 10.9) and the response of grateful human love to sovereign divine love (Galatians 2.20). This faith is, for Paul, the solitary badge of membership in God's people in **Christ**, marking them out in a way that **Torah**, and the works it prescribes, can never do.

Gehenna, hell

Gehenna is, literally, the valley of Hinnom, on the south-west slopes of Jerusalem. From ancient times it was used as a garbage dump, smouldering with a continual fire. Already by the time of Jesus some Jews used it as an image for the place of punishment after death. Jesus' own usage blends the two meanings in his warnings both to Jerusalem itself (unless it repents, the whole city will become a smouldering heap of garbage) and to people in general (to beware of God's final judgment).

149

Gentiles

The Jews divided the world into Jews and non-Jews. The Hebrew word for non-Jews, *goyim*, carries overtones both of family identity (i.e. not of Jewish ancestry) and of worship (i.e. of idols, not of the one true God YHWH). Though many Jews established good relations with Gentiles, not least in the Jewish Diaspora (the dispersion of Jews away from Palestine), officially there were taboos against contact such as intermarriage. In the New Testament the Greek word *ethne*, 'nations', carries the same meanings as *goyim*. Part of Paul's overmastering agenda was to insist that Gentiles who believed in Jesus had full rights in the Christian community alongside believing Jews, without having to become **circumcised**.

good news, gospel, message, word

The idea of 'good news', for which an older English word is 'gospel', had two principal meanings for first-century Jews. First, with roots in Isaiah, it meant the news of YHWH's long-awaited victory over evil and rescue of his people. Second, it was used in the Roman world of the accession, or birthday, or the emperor. Since for Jesus and Paul the announcement of God's inbreaking **kingdom** was both the fulfilment of prophecy and a challenge to the world's present rulers, 'gospel' became an important shorthand for both the message of Jesus himself, and the apostolic message about him. Paul saw this message as itself the vehicle of God's saving power (Romans 1.16; 1 Thessalonians 2.13).

The four canonical 'gospels' tell the story of Jesus in such a way as to bring out both these aspects (unlike some other so-called 'gospels' circulated in the second and subsequent centuries, which tended both to cut off the scriptural and Jewish roots of Jesus' achievement and to inculcate a private spirituality rather than confrontation with the world's rulers). Since in Isaiah this creative, life-giving good news was seen as God's own powerful word (40.8; 55.11), the early Christians could use 'word' or 'message' as another shorthand for the basic Christian proclamation.

gospel, *see* good news

heaven

Heaven is God's dimension of the created order (Genesis 1.1; Psalm 115.16; Matthew 6.9), whereas 'earth' is the world of space, time and matter that we know. 'Heaven' thus sometimes stands, reverentially, for 'God' (as in Matthew's regular '**kingdom** of heaven'). Normally hidden from human sight, heaven is occasionally revealed or unveiled so that people can see God's dimension of ordinary life (e.g. 2 Kings 6.17; Revelation 1, 4—5). Heaven in the New Testament is thus not usually seen as the place where God's people go after death; at the end the New Jerusalem descends *from* heaven *to* earth, joining the two dimensions for ever. 'Entering the kingdom of heaven' does not mean 'going to heaven after death', but belonging in the present to the people who steer their earthly course by the standards and purposes of heaven (cf. the Lord's Prayer: 'on earth as in heaven', Matthew 6. 10) and who are assured of membership in the **age to come**.

hell, *see* Gehenna

holy spirit

In Genesis 1.2, the spirit is God's presence and power *within* creation, without God being identified with creation. The same spirit entered people, notably the prophets, enabling them to speak and act for God. At his **baptism** by **John the Baptist**, Jesus was specially equipped with the spirit, resulting in his remarkable public career (Acts 10.38). After his **resurrection**, his followers were themselves filled (Acts 2) by the same spirit, now identified as Jesus' own spirit: the creator God was acting afresh, remaking the world and them too. The spirit enabled them to live out a holiness which the **Torah** could not, producing 'fruit' in their lives, giving them 'gifts' with which to serve God, the world, and the church, and assuring them of future resurrection (Romans 8; Galatians 4—5; 1 Corinthians 12—14). From very early in Christianity (e.g. Galatians 4.1–7), the spirit became part of the new revolutionary definition of God himself: 'the one who sends the son and the spirit of the son'.

John (the Baptist)

Jesus' cousin on his mother's side, born a few months before Jesus; his father was a **priest**. He acted as a prophet, baptizing in the Jordan – dramatically re-enacting the **Exodus** from Egypt – to prepare people, by **repentance**, for God's coming judgment. He may have had some contact with the **Essenes**, though his eventual public message was different from theirs. Jesus' own vocation was decisively confirmed at his **baptism** by John. As part of John's message of the **kingdom**, he outspokenly criticized Herod Antipas for marrying his brother's wife. Herod had him imprisoned, and then beheaded him at his wife's request (Mark 6.14–29). Groups of John's disciples continued a separate existence, without merging into Christianity, for some time afterwards (e.g. Acts 19.1–7).

justified, justification

God's declaration, from his position as judge of all the world, that someone is in the right, despite universal sin. This declaration will be made on the last day on the basis of an entire life (Romans 2.1–16), but is brought forward into the present on the basis of Jesus' achievement, because sin has been dealt with through his cross (Romans 3.21—4.25); the means of this present justification is simply **faith**. This means, particularly, that Jews and **Gentiles** alike are full members of the family promised by God to Abraham (Galatians 3; Romans 4).

kingdom of God, kingdom of heaven

Best understood as the king*ship*, or sovereign and saving rule, of Israel's God YHWH, as celebrated in several psalms (e.g. 99.1) and prophecies (e.g. Daniel 6.26f.). Because YHWH was the creator God, when he finally became king in the way he intended this would involve setting the world to rights, and particularly rescuing Israel from its enemies. 'Kingdom of God' and various equivalents (e.g. 'No king but God!') became revolutionary slogans around the time of Jesus. Jesus' own announcement of God's kingdom redefined these expectations around his own very different plan and vocation. His invitation to people to 'enter' the kingdom was a way of summoning them to allegiance to himself and his programme, seen as the start of God's long-awaited saving reign. For Jesus, the kingdom was coming not in a single move, but in stages, of which his own public career was one, his death and **resurrection** another, and a still future consummation another. Note that 'kingdom of **heaven**' is Matthew's preferred form for the same phrase, following a regular Jewish practice of saying 'heaven' rather than 'God'. It does not refer to a place ('heaven'), but to the fact of God's becoming king in and through Jesus and his achievement. Paul speaks of Jesus as **Messiah**, already in possession of his kingdom, waiting to hand it over finally to the father (1 Corinthians 15.23–28; cf. Ephesians 5.5).

law, *see* **Torah**

legal experts, lawyers, *see* **Pharisees**

life, soul, spirit
Ancient people held many different views about what made human beings the special creatures they are. Some, including many Jews, believed that to be complete, humans needed bodies as well as inner selves. Others, including many influenced by the philosophy of Plato (fourth century BC), believed that the important part of a human was the 'soul' (Gk: *psyche*), which at death would be happily freed from its bodily prison. Confusingly for us, the same word *psyche* is often used in the New Testament within a Jewish framework, where it clearly means 'life' or 'true self', without implying a body/soul dualism that devalues the body. Human inwardness of experience and understanding can also be referred to as 'spirit'. *See also* **holy spirit, resurrection.**

message, *see* **good news**

Messiah, messianic, Christ
The Hebrew word means literally 'anointed one', hence in theory either a prophet, **priest** or king. In Greek this translates as *Christos*; 'Christ' in early Christianity was a title, and only gradually became

an alternative proper name for Jesus. In practice 'Messiah' is mostly restricted to the notion, which took various forms in ancient Judaism, of the coming king who would be **David's** true heir, through whom YHWH would bring judgment to the world, and in particular would rescue Israel from pagan enemies. There was no single template of expectations. Scriptural stories and promises contributed to different ideals and movements, often focused on (a) decisive military defeat of Israel's enemies and (b) rebuilding or cleansing the **Temple**. The **Dead Sea Scrolls** speak of two 'Messiahs', one a priest and the other a king. The universal early Christian belief that Jesus was Messiah is only explicable, granted his crucifixion by the Romans (which would have been seen as a clear sign that he was not the Messiah), by their belief that God had raised him from the dead, so vindicating the implicit messianic claims of his earlier ministry.

miracles

Like some of the old prophets, notably Elijah and Elisha, Jesus performed many deeds of remarkable power, particularly healings. The **gospels** refer to these as 'deeds of power', 'signs', 'marvels' or 'paradoxes'. Our word 'miracle' tends to imply that God, normally 'outside' the closed system of the world, sometimes 'intervenes'; miracles have then frequently been denied as a matter of principle. However, in the Bible God is always present, however strangely, and 'deeds of power' are seen as *special* acts of a *present* God rather than as *intrusive* acts of an *absent* one. Jesus' own 'mighty works' are seen particularly, following prophecy, as evidence of his messiahship (e.g. Matthew 11.2–6).

Mishnah

The main codification of Jewish law (**Torah**) by the **rabbis**, produced in about AD 200, reducing to writing the 'oral Torah' which in Jesus' day ran parallel to the 'written Torah'. The Mishnah is itself the basis of the much larger collections of traditions in the two Talmuds (roughly AD 400).

parables

From the Old Testament onwards, prophets and other teachers used various story-telling devices as vehicles for their challenge to Israel (e.g. 2 Samuel 12.1–7). Sometimes these appeared as visions with interpretations (e.g. Daniel 7). Similar techniques were used by the **rabbis**. Jesus made his own creative adaptation of these traditions, in order to break open the world-view of his contemporaries and to invite them to share his vision of God's **kingdom** instead. His stories portrayed this as something that was *happening*, not just a timeless truth, and enabled his hearers to step inside the story and make it their own. As with some Old Testament visions, some of Jesus' parables have their own interpretations (e.g. the sower, Mark 4); others are thinly disguised retellings of the prophetic story of Israel (e.g. the wicked tenants, Mark 12).

parousia

Literally, it means 'presence', as opposed to 'absence', and is sometimes used by Paul with this sense (e.g. Philippians 2.12). It was already used in the Roman world for the ceremonial arrival of, for example, the emperor at a subject city or colony. Although the ascended Lord is not 'absent' from the church, when he 'appears' (Colossians 3.4; 1 John 3.2) in his 'second coming' this will be, in effect, an 'arrival' like that of the emperor, and Paul uses it thus in 1 Corinthians 15.23; 1 Thessalonians 2.19; etc. In the **gospels** it is found only in Matthew 24 (vv. 3, 27, 39).

Pharisees, legal experts, lawyers, rabbis

The Pharisees were an unofficial but powerful Jewish pressure group through most of the first centuries BC and AD. Largely lay-led, though including some **priests**, their aim was to purify Israel through intensified observance of the Jewish law (**Torah**), developing their own traditions about the precise meaning and application of scripture, their own patterns of prayer and other devotion, and their own calculations of the national hope. Though not all legal experts were Pharisees, most Pharisees were thus legal experts.

They effected a democratization of Israel's life, since for them the study and practice of Torah was equivalent to worshipping in the **Temple** – though they were adamant in pressing their own rules for the Temple liturgy on an unwilling (and often **Sadducean**) priesthood. This enabled them to survive AD 70 and, merging into the early rabbinic movement, to develop new ways forward. Politically they stood up for ancestral traditions, and were at the forefront of various movements of revolt against both pagan over-lordship and compromised Jewish leaders. By Jesus' day there were two distinct schools, the stricter one of Shammai, more inclined towards armed revolt, and the more lenient one of Hillel, ready to live and let live.

Jesus' debates with the Pharisees are at least as much a matter of agenda and policy (Jesus strongly opposed their separatist national-ism) as about details of theology and piety. Saul of Tarsus was a fervent right-wing Pharisee, presumably a Shammaite, until his conversion.

After the disastrous war of AD 66–70, these schools of Hillel and Shammai continued bitter debate on appropriate policy. Follow-ing the further disaster of AD 135 (the failed Bar-Kochba revolt against Rome), their traditions were carried on by the rabbis who, though looking to the earlier Pharisees for inspiration, developed a Torah-piety in which personal holiness and purity took the place of political agendas.

present age, age to come, eternal life

By the time of Jesus many Jewish thinkers divided history into two periods: 'the present age' and 'the age to come' – the latter being the time when YHWH would at last act decisively to judge evil, to rescue Israel, and to create a new world of justice and peace. The early Christians believed that, though the full blessings of the coming age lay still in the future, it had already begun with Jesus, particularly with his death and **resurrection**, and that by **faith** and **baptism** they were able to enter it already. 'Eternal life' does not mean simply 'existence continuing without end', but 'the life of the age to come'.

priests, high priest

Aaron, the older brother of Moses, was appointed Israel's first high priest (Exodus 28—29), and in theory his descendants were Israel's priests thereafter. Other members of his tribe (Levi) were 'Levites', performing other liturgical duties but not sacrificing. Priests lived among the people all around the country, having a local teaching role (Leviticus 10.11; Malachi 2.7), and going to Jerusalem by rotation to perform the **Temple** liturgy (e.g. Luke 2.8).

David appointed Zadok (whose Aaronic ancestry is sometimes questioned) as high priest, and his family remained thereafter the senior priests in Jerusalem, probably the ancestors of the **Sadducees**. One explanation of the origins of the **Qumran** Essenes is that they were a dissident group who believed themselves to be the rightful chief priests.

Qumran, *see* Dead Sea Scrolls

rabbis, *see* Pharisees

repentance

Literally, this means 'turning back'. It is widely used in the Old Testament and subsequent Jewish literature to indicate both a personal turning away from sin and Israel's corporate turning away from idolatry and back to YHWH. Through both meanings, it is linked to the idea of 'return from **exile**'; if Israel is to 'return' in all senses, it must 'return' to YHWH. This is at the heart of the summons of both **John the Baptist** and Jesus. In Paul's writings it is mostly used for **Gentiles** turning away from idols to serve the true God; also for sinning Christians who need to return to Jesus.

resurrection

In most biblical thought, human bodies matter and are not merely disposable prisons for the **soul**. When ancient Israelites wrestled with the goodness and justice of YHWH, the creator, they ultimately came to insist that he must raise the dead (Isaiah 26.19; Daniel 12.2–3) – a suggestion firmly resisted by classical pagan thought.

The longed-for return from **exile** was also spoken of in terms of YHWH raising dry bones to new **life** (Ezekiel 37.1–14). These ideas were developed in the second-**Temple** period, not least at times of martyrdom (e.g. 2 Maccabees 7). Resurrection was not just 'life after death', but a newly embodied life *after* 'life after death'; those at present dead were either 'asleep', or seen as 'souls', 'angels' or 'spirits', awaiting new embodiment.

The early Christian belief that Jesus had been raised from the dead was not that he had 'gone to **heaven**', or that he had been 'exalted', or was 'divine'; they believed all those as well, but each could have been expressed without mention of resurrection. Only the bodily resurrection of Jesus explains the rise of the early church, particularly its belief in Jesus' messiahship (which his crucifixion would have called into question). The early Christians believed that they themselves would be raised to a new, transformed bodily life at the time of the Lord's return or **parousia** (e.g. Philippians 3.20f.).

sabbath

The Jewish sabbath, the seventh day of the week, was a regular reminder both of creation (Genesis 2.3; Exodus 20.8–11) and of the **Exodus** (Deuteronomy 5.15). Along with **circumcision** and the food laws, it was one of the badges of Jewish identity within the pagan world of late antiquity, and a considerable body of Jewish **law** and custom grew up around its observance.

sacrifice

Like all ancient people, the Israelites offered animal and vegetable sacrifices to their God. Unlike others, they possessed a highly detailed written code (mostly in Leviticus) for what to offer and how to offer it; this in turn was developed in the **Mishnah** (*c.* AD 200). The Old Testament specifies that sacrifices can only be offered in the Jerusalem **Temple**; after this was destroyed in AD 70, sacrifices ceased, and Judaism developed further the idea, already present in some teachings, of prayer, fasting and almsgiving as alternative forms of sacrifice. The early Christians used the language of sacrifice in connection with such things as holiness, evangelism and the **eucharist**.

Sadducees

By Jesus' day, the Sadducees were the aristocracy of Judaism, possibly tracing their origins to the family of Zadok, **David**'s **high priest**. Based in Jerusalem, and including most of the leading priestly families, they had their own traditions and attempted to resist the pressure of the **Pharisees** to conform to theirs. They claimed to rely only on the Pentateuch (the first five books of the Old Testament), and denied any doctrine of a future life, particularly of the **resurrection** and other ideas associated with it, presumably because of the encouragement such beliefs gave to revolutionary movements. No writings from the Sadducees have survived, unless the apocryphal book of Ben Sirach ('Ecclesiasticus') comes from them. The Sadducees themselves did not survive the destruction of Jerusalem and the **Temple** in AD 70.

the satan, 'the accuser', demons

The Bible is never very precise about the identity of the figure known as 'the satan'. The Hebrew word means 'the accuser', and at times the satan seems to be a member of YHWH's heavenly council, with special responsibility as director of prosecutions (1 Chronicles 21.1; Job 1—2; Zechariah 3.1f.). However, it becomes identified variously with the serpent of the garden of Eden (Genesis 3.1–15) and with the rebellious daystar cast out of **heaven** (Isaiah 14.12–15), and was seen by many Jews as the quasi-personal source of evil standing behind both human wickedness and large-scale injustice, sometimes operating through semi-independent 'demons'. By Jesus' time various words were used to denote this figure, including Beelzebul/b (lit. 'Lord of the flies') and simply 'the evil one'; Jesus warned his followers against the deceits this figure could perpetrate. His opponents accused him of being in league with the satan, but the early Christians believed that Jesus in fact defeated it both in his own struggles with temptation (Matthew 4; Luke 4), his exorcisms of demons, and his death (1 Corinthians 2.8; Colossians 2.15). Final victory over this ultimate enemy is thus assured (Revelation 20), though the struggle can still be fierce for Christians (Ephesians 6.10–20).

scribes

In a world where many could not write, or not very well, a trained class of writers ('scribes') performed the important function of drawing up contracts for business, marriage, etc. Many would thus be legal experts, and quite possibly **Pharisees**, though being a scribe was compatible with various political and religious standpoints. The work of Christian scribes was of vital importance in copying early Christian writings, particularly the stories about Jesus.

son of David, David's son

An alternative, and infrequently used, title for **Messiah**. The messianic promises of the Old Testament often focus specifically on David's son, for example 2 Samuel 7.12–16; Psalm 89.19–37. Joseph, Mary's husband, is called 'son of David' by the angel in Matthew 1.20.

son of God

Originally a title for Israel (Exodus 4.22) and the Davidic king (Psalm 2.7); also used of ancient angelic figures (Genesis 6.2). By the New Testament period it was already used as a **messianic** title, for example in the **Dead Sea Scrolls**. There, and when used of Jesus in the **gospels** (e.g. Matthew 16.16), it means, or reinforces, 'Messiah', without the later significance of 'divine'. However, already in Paul the transition to the fuller meaning (one who was already equal with God and was sent by him to become human and to become Messiah) is apparent, without loss of the meaning 'Messiah' itself (e.g. Galatians 4.4).

soul, *see* life

spirit, *see* life, holy spirit

Temple

The Temple in Jerusalem was planned by **David** (*c.* 1000 BC) and built by his son Solomon as the central sanctuary for all Israel. After reforms under Hezekiah and Josiah in the seventh century BC, it was destroyed by Babylon in 587 BC. Rebuilding by the returned **exiles** began in 538 BC, and was completed in 516, initiating the 'second-Temple period'. Judas Maccabaeus cleansed it in 164 BC after its desecration by Antiochus Epiphanes (167). Herod the Great began to rebuild and beautify it in 19 BC; the work was completed in AD 63. The Temple was destroyed by the Romans in AD 70. Many Jews believed it should and would be rebuilt; some still do. The Temple was not only the place of **sacrifice**; it was believed to be the unique dwelling of YHWH on earth, the place where **heaven** and earth met.

Torah, Jewish law

'Torah', narrowly conceived, consists of the first five books of the Old Testament, the 'five books of Moses' or 'Pentateuch'. (These contain much law, but also much narrative.) It can also be used for the whole Old Testament scriptures, though strictly these are the 'law, prophets and writings'. In a broader sense, it refers to the whole developing corpus of Jewish legal tradition, written and oral; the oral Torah was initially codified in the **Mishnah** around AD 200, with wider developments found in the two Talmuds, of Babylon and Jerusalem, codified around AD 400. Many Jews in the time of Jesus and Paul regarded the Torah as being so strongly God-given as to be almost itself, in some sense, divine; some (e.g. Ben Sirach 24) identified it with the figure of 'Wisdom'. Doing what Torah said was not seen as a means of earning God's favour, but rather of expressing gratitude, and as a key badge of Jewish identity.

word, *see* good news

YHWH

The ancient Israelite name for God, from at least the time of the **Exodus** (Exodus 6.2f.). It may originally have been pronounced 'Yahweh', but by the time of Jesus it was considered too holy to speak out loud, except by the **high priest** once a year in the Holy of Holies in the **Temple**. Instead, when reading scripture, pious Jews would say *Adonai*, 'Lord', marking this usage by adding the vowels of *Adonai* to the consonants of YHWH, eventually producing the hybrid 'Jehovah'. The word YHWH is formed from the verb 'to be', combining 'I am who I am', 'I will be who I will be', and perhaps 'I am because I am', emphasizing YHWH's sovereign creative power.